SECRETS OF THE JUNGLE:

Lessons on Survival and Success
in Today's Organizations

Shirley Peddy, Ph.D

learningconnections
Corpus Christi, Texas

The organizations, tribes and characters in this book are either the product of the author's imagination or a combination of many people and many experiences in many organizations. Any resemblance to a specific company, tribe or individual is purely coincidental.

ISBN 0-9651376-0-0

Printed in the United State of America
at Morgan Printing in Austin, Texas
Graphics and book design by Outsource Graphics in Houston, Texas
Printing 1 2 3 4 5 6 7 8 9 10

To Red Peddy,

**my husband, mentor and friend
whose love and support make all
things possible.**

Acknowledgment

To acknowledge a debt is not to pay it, but merely to admit you owe it. In this context, I owe so much to the people who provided both content and emotional support for this venture. Some participated actively; others helped to lay a foundation over the years.

I am deeply indebted to George V. Sherman, Jr. who is sure to find himself, his ideas and his good advice scattered throughout the story. He has been a champion editor and a strong ally. I am enriched for having known and worked with him.

A special thanks to my good friends Dave Radcliffe, Dianne Burns, Nigel Bristow, Tom McNally and Susan Buddeke, who took the time to read the book and offered their ideas and encouragement, and to Sue Howe, whose urging played a key role in my starting this project.

I would like to express my gratitude to Gene Dalton, whose good opinion of my work has been a continuing source of inspiration.

Jack and Barbara Moccabee started out as business associates. Their company, Outsource Graphics, is responsible for the cover and design of this book. But they went much further. They became advocates and partners in putting it together, and I can't thank them enough for all their help.

I also owe a debt of gratitude to my friend and minister, Howard Caesar, who read the story and went the extra mile for me. His support and good wishes meant a lot.

I have been very fortunate in my career, having the opportunity to work with some successful and wise colleagues. To them I owe the insights and secrets contained in this book. Many thanks to Pat Mulva, Vince Hennessey, Dick Francis, Pat Hewlett, Donald Doggett, Jim Herring and Dan Muschalik. A special note of appreciation to Courtney Rogers and all my friends at Novations. I appreciate our relationship and your continuing interest in my success.

My heartfelt thanks to my sister, Jody Heymann, the most generous person I've ever known. She has been a fan, a critic and a wonderful confidante through this entire project. Thanks also to her husband, and my friend, Dr. Hans Heymann, whose good wishes and praise meant so much to me.

And finally, my deepest gratitude to my dearest friend and greatest supporter, my husband Red Peddy, who introduced me to the rainforest, who read every line of the book a dozen times and who continues to be there when I need him.

Contents

"Come to the edge," he said.
They said, "We are afraid."
"Come to the edge," he said.
They came.
He pushed them...
And they flew.
...Guillaume Apollinaire

PROLOGUE

The Difference Between Torches and Lamps

Once there were two friends who worked for the same company. Both had MBAs and both were intelligent and ambitious. Jack had worked for Perry Winkle Enterprises for eighteen years. Sandra had been there for seven. Although they were in different roles, they even reported to the same manager, Bill Jameson. But there the similarity ended. In fact, if you talked to Jack or Sandra, you might think they worked for different companies. Jack was happy at PWE. People at every level and from all over the company sought his advice, asked for his help and included him in their most important projects.

Sandra was unhappy. She worked hard, but she didn't feel appreciated. She was so busy working that she didn't have time to get involved in the work others were doing. And people realized that. They thought of Sandra as hard working, dependable and prompt, but they never thought of her when they wanted advice or help with their most important projects.

Late one afternoon, she stopped by Jack's office. "I came to say good-bye, Jack. I'm on my way to Bill's office to drop this letter off. It's my resignation, dated tomorrow. Before I go, I wonder if you would mind if I asked you something. I know you must be very busy -- but..."

"Of course I wouldn't mind," said Jack, his voice full of concern. He had played a part in recruiting Sandra, and he was disappointed she was thinking of leaving.

"You seem so happy here at PWE. Everyone notices the work you do. You don't ask for it, but you seem to get a lot of credit and appreciation. I don't understand what you do to get all this approval. You don't work harder than I do, yet everyone asks your opinion. PWE managers who won't give me a minute come to your office just to 'kick things around.' I know I must have done something wrong, but I can't figure out what it is." Her eyes welled with tears.

"I'm sorry you've been unhappy," said Jack, passing Sandra a handful of tissues. He paused for a moment as she dabbed her eyes, then continued, "I don't think you've done anything wrong, but if you've set your sights on approval, perhaps you've been aiming at the wrong target. *Management approval is elusive -- and even if you hit the mark, it doesn't last very long.* You asked me how I did it. Well, here's my secret. *Once I forgot about making an impression and set my sights on making a difference, everything began to fall into place.*

"I know you're discouraged, Sandra," he continued, "but look at it this way -- you have discovered what many never learn: Hard work just isn't enough. *I'm not suggesting that you work harder but that you approach work in another way.* Let me illustrate with an analogy. In business, some people are torches and some are lamps. Both are sources of light, but the difference is important. Torches use up their own fuel and burn out while lamps are plugged into a continuously renewing energy source."

"I see what you mean," said Sandra. "Maybe I've been operating more like a torch than a lamp. But what can I do?"

Jack thought for a moment. "You're a talented person," he said, "and you do work hard at PWE. *That entitles you to a paycheck and the opportunity to continue working here, but it won't earn you the other rewards you describe.* I'll answer your question no matter what you decide, but if you stay with PWE at least six months longer, I'll teach you the secrets I've learned over the years."

So Sandra decided to stay and with Jack's help, she too became a lamp that shone throughout the company. This is Sandra's story…and possibly yours.

Jack had been intrigued by the jungle since college, when undecided about his future, he had taken a year off to see the world and had spent the better part of it with a biologist friend in the tropical rain forests of the Amazon. The jungle had taught him many lessons. There were rules for survival there and secrets for traveling it successfully. Over time, he had come to realize such rules and secrets also exist in organizations. He was writing a book about these parallels and invited Sandra to read and comment on it. This is how she learned most of the rules and all of the secrets that changed her life.

> "Learning is not attained by chance.
> It must be sought for with ardor
> And attended to with diligence."
> ....Abigail Adams

THE FIRST LESSON

On Learning, Mentors and Tests

Jack's book, *Secrets of the Jungle*, began...

The Elder

The road was overgrown with foliage. I could not find the path. My foot caught in the tangled roots of a mangrove tree and I stumbled. My elbow was skinned and bloody. I could taste panic rising in my throat. Suddenly I felt a warm, callused hand on my arm, helping me up. That was my first meeting with the Elder. I looked into kind brown eyes.

"Are you lost?" he asked, his voice gentle and concerned.

I felt lost. Almost two years had passed since I had left the city behind me and returned to the Korios tribe. Somehow, everything was different than I had imagined it would be. I was an outsider. When I tried to find out what was wrong, people told me not to worry -- I would find my place. I knew better. When others spoke at the tribal meetings, the chiefs would listen, but if I asked a question or made a suggestion, I could sense their hesitance, hear them shuffling their feet, see them nodding to each other as if to confirm something they had said outside of my hearing. I didn't understand what was going on, but I was sure of one thing, I didn't fit in.

I was confused. I didn't know which way to turn or what to do. I had walked for hours that day searching for the answer when I lost my way and fell. And so I told the Elder my story. He listened, asked questions and listened some more. He understood my words, but more than that, he understood the anxiety and fear beneath them. After that, we talked many times. And so my life changed. He taught me about the jungle: how to understand it, how to survive in it and how to honor the lessons it taught me. And he started with the first rule: *"If you would know the secrets of the jungle, you must dedicate yourself to learning."*

"Learning what?" I asked.

"...learning how to find the secrets and how to use them effectively for your good and the good of the tribe. In so doing, you will set out on a path that leads to contribution, and you will earn the respect of the chiefs. Then when you speak at the tribal meetings, all will listen."

"I *have* learned," I protested. "I spent many years in school. I want to practice what I know."

"Patience," he told me. "Never believe you know all there is to know about the jungle, for when you do, you will be prey to its hidden dangers. What do you know of the jungle terrain?"

"I have seen the lianas wrapped around giant trees climbing toward the sun and the pond rich with red-eyed frogs. I've stood in the darkness of the forest where there is no light and I've seen the sunrise above the hill."

"Where have you seen these things?" he asked.

"Not far from here," I replied.

"So you have traveled in one part of the jungle?"

"Yes," I replied, "only one. But I have heard my teachers speak of the black caimans that live in the rivers and eat the tree frogs -- and waters alive with tall red and white birds with long necks -- and flesh-eating fish."

14

"Yes, my son," he said, "what you have seen for yourself and learned from others is only the beginning of your education. In school you proved your ability to learn. You were trained by people who studied and learned about jungles and passed this information on to you; but most have never lived or worked in this jungle. Like me and every guide you will ever have, their perspective is limited. *What you have gained in school is the privilege to join the tribe and learn.*"

"The jungle is a living system. It can be hostile; it can be indifferent; or it can be friendly; but whatever it is, it's a place of challenge -- of danger and of opportunity. To survive in it, you must learn its secrets. Those who ignore the dangers will run into hostile tribes, ferocious animals, and unfriendly territory. Those who take the time to learn about it will be rewarded by it."

Sandra could see how business might be like the jungle with its surprises and challenges. She turned to Jack, "But how do you learn these things?"

"In school you learned by reading books, listening to lectures, and asking questions. From time to time you were tested to be sure you could repeat the information to the satisfaction of your teachers."

"In business there are also schools. But you will learn most from the informal system: by paying attention to experienced people who know the secrets, working with others who are successful and listening to their stories and by profiting from both praise and criticism. *Remember, you are constantly being tested. To pass, you must earn the respect of the people you work with, and, at the same time, treat them with respect whether you think they have earned it or not. Some people fail the test because they don't produce results, but more fail it because they don't understand the importance of building good working relationships with others.*"

"I get along with my peers. And Bill seems to like me, even if he ignores me most of the time."

"That's a start. But getting along is not enough. You need to establish friendships and relationships if you want to learn the 'secrets of the organizational jungle.' In business, your teachers are everywhere. They are the people who bring you the mail and the people who make financial decisions. They are the people who ask for your help and those who have high expectations of you. Some you will like; some you won't. Problems come when you don't recognize the people around you as your teachers and the opportunities and challenges they bring as tests."

"If my teachers are everyone, why use an Elder in the story?"

"This is a book about being successful in the world of business. In order to do that you must learn the rules and have someone who can whisper these secrets to you. What is an Elder but a person wise in the ways of the jungle, a spokesperson, a teacher, a confidante and a guide. In my eighteen years of organizational life I have been guided by many Elders."

"But can't you learn these things by yourself?" asked Sandra. "I mean, aren't there successful people who have never had a mentor?"

"Probably are. Some people learn the rules intuitively. Most don't. Someone once gave me this analogy: you can learn to hit a golf ball by going to a driving range and hitting a million balls, or you can take lessons from the pros. Which do you think makes the most sense?"

Sandra laughed. "Or you can sit in your office and wonder how other people get such great scores. So, what kinds of things did the 'pros' teach you?"

"Let me give you a couple of examples. Mary, was a well-respected manager. *She taught me the importance of finishing what I start.* She spoke of someone who continuously brought her his problems. *'I don't need anyone to find problems for me. I can identify enough problems in a day to keep me busy for a year,'* she said. 'What I am looking for are solutions. If you have a problem and a solution, come see me.'"

"Does that mean you should never bring someone a problem unless you know the answer? Wouldn't that keep problems swept under the carpet and prevent people from correcting what's wrong?"

16

"That's a good point, Sandra. No, I don't think Mary meant that you shouldn't alert others to problems. What I think she meant is, if you encounter a problem, don't be too quick to hand it off. That makes you appear weak and powerless. Try to solve it first. At the very least, come up with some recommendations. Then be sure to tell the boss what steps you have already taken. She'll appreciate your efforts, believe me."

"Mary also told me a secret that is among the hardest to learn and most important to remember: not to confuse criticism of my work for criticism of me. I remember the occasion well. My supervisor had written a comment on something I did, and I was sure he was wrong. I regarded it as a personal attack and was very offended by it. Mary was sympathetic. 'Write him a note,' she offered, 'and clarify your position.' So I wrote the note and asked Mary what she thought of it. 'Let's take personalities out of it,' she said and suggested one edit that I'll never forget. I had written the sentence, 'I'd like to point out why I disagree with you.' Mary crossed out the words *with you.* Then I read it over: 'I'd like to point out why I disagree.' It softened the tone. Mary agreed. *'If you want to get things resolved, center your attention on the problem, not on the person.* You've probably heard the old saying, 'You can always disagree without being disagreeable.'"

"Was Mary your Mentor?"

"Yes," said Jack, "one of them."

That is the second rule of the jungle: *Be guided by the wisdom of others until others seek you out to learn what you know."*

"But who are these others and why should they be interested in me?"

"In the book Keli asks the Elder the same question. Here's the passage. Read his answer and tell me what you think."

"Look beyond position in the tribe and see others as people. In the jungle, we know that everyone is connected to the earth -- and to each other. I know another through the things he keeps around him, what he talks about in the tribal meetings, the actions he takes. Therefore, in your quest

for knowledge, choose those whose wisdom can guide you. Then use your powers of observation to find the connection."

Looking up from the manuscript, Sandra nodded. "So you look at the pictures in their offices or things they keep on their desks or listen to their casual conversation to see what you have in common. Is that what you mean?"

"That's it," said Jack. "Sometimes you've been to the same places or you know some of the same people or your children go to the same school or you have similar hobbies. Once you find something you can talk about, whether it's business or social, it's easier to make a connection. I remember starting a conversation with one manager about his newly decorated office. It's that simple. Refine your powers of observation and be a good listener. That's the key."

"I guess it helps if you're a golfer or enjoy football."

"It might, but don't focus on that. I've known a lot of successful men and women who couldn't swing a club or a racket and preferred the symphony to football."

"I was once assigned a mentor," said Sandra. "That didn't work out. After a while, I decided we just couldn't communicate. We had nothing to talk about. Finding a good mentor isn't easy. And getting someone interested in you beyond a superficial level is even harder. Once you found the connection, how did you do it?"

Closing his eyes, Jack reflected. Then he smiled. "It's like finding a friend. *Assigned mentors can help, but the best relationships are based on choice and built on liking, trust and reciprocity."*

"Reciprocity?"

"Yes, Sandra. In every relationship there must be something in it for both people. That's why assigned mentoring may be helpful, but it's not as lasting. And don't think you don't have a lot to offer another person. Being a good listener, giving honest feedback, providing information, even giving advice -- there are all sorts of things you can do. In one role I was in, it was my job to find speakers for communication programs. You'd be surprised how many executives welcomed the opportunity to speak to a group of attentive participants."

Sandra leaned forward in her chair. "So, you decide who you want to mentor you. Then what?"

"You already know one way to start a mentoring relationship: ask for advice about something. Isn't that how you and I got together? That is the sincerest of all compliments because it implies respect. There are other ways as well. Mary was a manager in the Controller's Department. We worked on a project together, and we just liked each other from the start. Dean was my boss' boss. I used to drop by his office to say hello. When I changed jobs, I stopped by his office to say good-bye. He said, 'Stay in touch,' and I did just that. He turned out to be one of the best mentors I ever had."

"It sounds like you made it happen. I mean, do mentors ever find you?"

"Sure. It's like any other relationship. You just click with some people and …."

"I know," said Sandra. "I'm just beginning to understand how torches become lamps. They need to be connected to a source -- like a mentor. Right?"

"It's a good beginning! *One thing I've learned, in business as in life, relationships count.* Having people who care about you is one of the greatest of all satisfactions and can sustain you in rough times. Mentors do make a difference. Just don't rely on them as a substitute for performance."

"Developing mentoring relationships takes time," he continued. "In your first year or two what you really need is a strong and patient coach, someone who can help you learn the way things work. This can be a supervisor, a peer or almost anyone. I remember when I first came to PWE. I had worked somewhere else before, and it was like crossing the border into another country. What I needed most then was a teacher and a translator, someone who could introduce me to the customs and help me interpret the language. I was lucky. My first mentor was the person who hired me. I remember how I used to go into Carla's office, close the door, and ask questions about how to fill out an expense account, what to call people in higher positions, what to wear to a PWE off-site meeting and how to interpret events that had happened in a meeting I attended."

"After I had been there for awhile, I needed someone to 'clue me in.' Who were the people I needed to know? What other resources should I develop? That person functioned more like a guide. Mary played that role, and she gave me the feedback that helped me become a better listener," he chuckled, "and a whole lot less defensive."

"Later, my mentor was more a supporter, a friend -- someone I could laugh with, confide in and who shared my interests. Dean sponsored me several times in major projects. He knew the players and he knew the game. When I needed funds that had not been budgeted, he knew how to find them. When he retired, I felt the loss, as did others he had mentored."

"There were several others who mentored me. They were sources of valuable information. Many times I learned about reorganizations and other important changes the company was planning before they were announced."

"How come people were willing to tell you?"

"Because they trusted me and because I always followed certain rules, Sandra."

"But how did you know what the rules were?"

"Some I learned from peers. Some from observation. I just understood that most people long to be helpful, but they don't want to be harmed in the process. *It takes a long time to establish trust, and a very short time to destroy it.* The rules are universal, and if you think about them, they make a lot of sense. People will tell you things if you follow them, but once you violate them -- well, it's all over."

"So, tell me, what are they?"

"I was just listing them to include in *Secrets,*" said Jack reaching into his pocket. Sandra unfolded the paper and read what Jack had written.

■ Thank people privately and acknowledge their worth publicly.

■ Build trust by being honest about your motives.

■ Never break a confidence or tell anyone the source of your information.

■ Never use another person to your advantage for even in mentoring relationships, we are tested to see if we are worthy."

"I like your list," said Sandra, "but I'm not sure I understand what kind of tests you're referring to."

"Let me give you an example. I remember one time when I had gone in to ask Mary for advice. I was on a project team with Mike Arnold, and I was sure I was doing more than my share. I went to Hank, my supervisor, who suggested I tell Mike's boss. I wasn't sure. As I described the situation to Mary, I became exasperated and told her, 'Mike is taking advantage of me. I don't like working with him because he's not a team player. He's too busy looking out for himself.' I was really getting worked up, but Mary's facial expression stopped me cold. 'I wonder if you know that Mike has a sick child at home,' she told me. 'I know Mike, and I'm sure he would want to know the situation he has put you in. He's a good person, Jack. So are you. If you have a problem working together, the best way to handle that is with him...privately.'"

"And that's what I did," continued Jack. "But I learned a very important secret from that encounter."

Sandra nodded, "*Never put another person down.* Right?"

21

"Right. And after that I never did. But I have seen it done in meetings and noted the exchange of glances since then. It may hurt the one you talk about, but the real arrows come back to you."

That evening Sandra started a journal to capture the key ideas from each lesson.

Sandra's Journal

The First Lesson

To survive, recognize the tests and the teachers.
To succeed, learn, learn, learn.
The secret is, find and develop mentors.

THE SECOND LESSON

On Perceptions and Attitude

"Jack, can I see you right away?" It was Sandra's voice on the telephone and she sounded shaky.

"I've got a one o'clock meeting. It shouldn't take more than an hour. Can I call you then?"

An audible sigh, "Okay."

It couldn't wait. Jack knew that instinctively. "Want to grab a bite of lunch with me? It's got to be in the cafeteria, but we could find a quiet table. You don't have much time to decide. I'm leaving right now."

He could hear the smile in her voice. "See you there. And Jack, thanks."

She was sitting at a table in the corner with only a glass of water and an apple in front of her.

"Is that your normal lunch?" he asked. "Keep this up and you'll blow away before I finish the book."

"I just couldn't eat now, Jack. The apple is for later."

"What's on your mind?"

"I just had a performance review with Bill. It was awful. I don't know if I should pack my bags now or not."

"Please don't. It's only been two weeks since you read Chapter One. Do you want to tell me what he said?"

"He basically sees me as average. Average! After all my long hours and hard work! I felt like crying -- or throwing his desk at him. He says I understand my job and I do that well, but I don't have the big picture. We had quite a disagreement about that. I think I reacted pretty strongly because I was so taken aback by what he said. And at the end of it, well, he told me I should 'lighten up.'"

"Don't pack your bags. 'Average' is not what you are, but clearly, it's Bill's perception of you. And since you didn't cry or throw the desk at him, you can put that in the win column. Look, Sandra, you're angry and you need time to think about this. I'd like to give you the next piece of the story. It touches on feedback and perceptions. Maybe it will help. Then, when you've finished it, we could get together and strategize a bit. What do you say?"

"I'm willing to do anything that will help."

"And, Sandra, don't think this is the end of the world. Early in my career I had a similar episode with a supervisor. He saw me as 'creative but undisciplined.' He felt that I let things 'slip' if I didn't find them important. He said I was 'unfocused' and a few other things that escape me. My first reaction was just like yours. I wanted to leap over the desk and -- My career was over! I thought of quitting. Why hang around and die slowly. I talked with Carla about it. You remember Carla. She's the person who coached me when I first came to PWE. Anyway, I stormed into her office, shut the door and unloaded. She listened and then she told me a similar story about an appraisal someone gave her. Then she added, 'The funny thing about it was, when I thought it over later, I could see some truth in what my supervisor said. I didn't like to hear it, and I didn't particularly like the way he said it, but he was right. *The most important thing,' she said, 'is not to attack the messenger because then, the messages stop*, or they get couched in such ambiguous language that they're indecipherable.' Get what I mean?"

"So that's why you say it's a good thing I didn't throw the desk at Bill."

"Right!" He looked at his watch. "Gotta run. Will you come by at two or would you rather I brought the chapter to your office?"

"I'd rather come by yours. Right now I'm not much in the mood to stay in my office. I've got a little time. I think I'll take a couple of laps around the building."

"Good for you. See you later."

When Sandra left work that night she had Chapter Two in hand. With Steve on a business trip, it would be a quiet evening, a good night for reading.

The Spirit of Learning

My first meeting with the Elder had given me a lot to think about. In his quiet and gentle way he had let me know that I had much to learn. But where should I start? I wanted to belong more than anything, to feel accepted by the tribe. I felt the need to talk to him. When I went to his house to see him, I was disappointed at his absence. I walked to the pond where he often met with the other Elders, but he was not there. Someone told me he was sitting by the river. I found him there cutting into the brown roots of the cassava with a strange-looking knife.

"What is that?" I asked.

"It is a knife, a gift from the toolmaker, Lutar. Isn't it a fine tool! Lutar made it from the jaw of a peccary, a water pig. I shall now have no trouble peeling the fruit to eat." He offered me some of the root, and we ate in silence.

"You are troubled," he said.

"How did you know?"

"It is written on your face, in your eyes, in the down turn of your mouth. How would I not know?"

"I don't know where to begin," I said. "I am unhappy. Nothing is working out."

"Begin with all you search for."

"I want to belong, to be accepted. I want to have a name that others recognize and call. I want things to do that make me feel useful. I want to be part of the laughter, and not the one others laugh at; I want Toolmakers like Lutar to carve a knife and give it to me as a gift; and I want to walk inside any hut and be as welcome as you are."

"That is a good list. You shall have all that. Now tell me, my son, what have you given?"

I shook my head. "Father, I have nothing to give. That is the problem."

"But you are of value," he replied. "*You must give of yourself.*"

"I don't understand."

"*Start by adopting a spirit of learning. That is a commitment to be worthy.*"

"But how will that help me? No one but you will know."

"Nor should they. For then you are only describing a wish. Do not speak of commitment for it is best revealed by actions. *You must be willing to be helpful without gratitude, eager to volunteer without reward, and able to accept criticism without anger.* All of these acts will be noticed."

"What will I gain?"

"More than you give. Keli, why did you return to the Korios?"

"I was born a Korio. My mother told me she had left the tribe and moved to the city to support me when my father died. She always kept our customs and told me many stories about the tribe. I never felt at home in the city. From the beginning, I knew I would return to the village someday and live with my people. I came back two years ago, but I don't feel as if I belong."

"Keli, you are a member of the tribe. But you are seen as uncommitted. You do not go out of your way for others. You have not chosen a path. You walk into the jungle alone. You do not ask for what you need."

I hung my head. "I cannot hear this," I said.

He reached out and touched my shoulder. "My son, if you cannot hear this, I cannot help you."

I looked up. There were tears in his eyes. I was overwhelmed.

"Today there is a meeting," he said. "We will be choosing some of the tribal members to help plan a celebration for the Tribal Chief's birthday. Shall I tell them you have volunteered to help?"

"Please," I responded.

"Will you accept any part, no matter how small?"

"I will," I said eagerly.

"It is done."

Sandra looked up from the memo she was writing. Jack was standing in the doorway to her office. "Sorry I didn't call. I was in the neighborhood. Feel like being interrupted?"

"I do. And before you ask, yes, I'm feeling better."

"Good. What did you think of Chapter Two?"

"I haven't finished reading it yet, but what I did read gave me some things to think about. There were two parts that really struck me. One was when the Elder told Keli, if you can't accept feedback, then I can't help you. I guess that's one of the areas I need to work on -- big time."

"Don't feel bad about it, Sandra. Most people aren't very good at giving feedback and few of us have enough self-esteem to be open to it, especially when it is delivered imperfectly, which it usually is. *It helps to think of yourself as a business and feedback as information.*

You're Sandra, Inc., a company that wants to remain profitable, so you periodically survey your customers to see how the business is doing. Research shows that most customers of a business don't complain, even though they may be dissatisfied. They just switch to another supplier. Those who do complain or criticize often become its most loyal advocates. So it's to Sandra, Inc.'s benefit to understand how her customers see her so she can improve. Bill Jameson is your chief customer and he has given you his perspective. He says you are 'average.' That part is not too helpful. But he has told you a couple of specific things. He says you 'don't understand the big picture,' for one. The other is 'lighten up.' Let's start with the first one. Okay?"

"Suits me."

"What's your guess as to why he thinks you don't understand the big picture?"

"I don't need to guess, Jack. He told me in so many words. He said I don't get out of my office and meet people. In fact he implied I have a sign in my office that says, 'State your business -- fast.' He said I'm so wrapped up in what I'm doing that I don't seem available for other projects. He reminded me that when he was looking for a volunteer for the bond drive, I was polite, but disinterested. I told him I have been hard at work on projects with short deadlines, but he brushed that off as if it were unimportant. He said, there have been other opportunities to volunteer, and I've rejected every one of them. I guess I'm feeling very undervalued, Jack."

"It sounds to me as if you're underutilized too. How much of what Bill says fits?"

She hesitated, took a deep breath and blurted out, "All of it! I guess that's why I'm so angry. Why didn't he tell me it would impact my career? Why did he wait until my review?"

"He should have told you. But now he has, and that's the important thing. Bill's a good guy. He may be stating his own opinion, or he may be reflecting things he's heard from others. Now you know what's on his mind, you can come up with a plan that takes you out of your office and into the middle of what's going on."

"I can do that. My problem is, I'm having trouble understanding what the fuss is about."

"It's about commitment, Sandra. And it's vitally important. Let me explain. There are basically five levels of commitment at work. At the lowest level are the people who come to work every day, put in their eight hours and go home. For some, that's what a job is - a place to go to earn money to support themselves and their families. No more, no less. Their commitment is to their paychecks -- and the company realizes that. It gets a fair amount of work from them, but the level of commitment is mutually low."

"Then there are the people who are committed to the job as a means to an end. That's the next level. This can take several directions -- as a stepping stone to personal growth, or as a means to advance their own agenda. Those who use it for their own growth usually don't plan to stay. They see their present job as an interim move toward what they may really want. Those who work their own agenda focus only on what makes them look good. If they can hand their work over to another or fail to do it, it's okay as long as the boss doesn't find out. If you ever inherit a job from one of those folks, you wind up with a mess of things that have fallen through the cracks. In either case, the commitment is to self and as far as the organization is concerned, it tends to be short term."

"I've known a couple of people like that," said Sandra. "They are eager to get your help but reluctant to give theirs. In time, everyone catches on."

"Right. Now the third level is made up of people committed to their professions. They provide the organization an excellent service. When the organization no longer satisfies their needs or *vice versa*, they move on. The commitment on both sides is a business transaction, a *quid pro quo*."

"The fourth level is people who are committed to the work or the work product. You give them a job and they do it, and they ask for more. They don't get out or around too much because they are too busy doing the work of several people. The organization may appreciate their work but often overlooks their personal contributions when it comes to handing out rewards. It's a narrow view I admit, and I'm not saying it's fair, but I've heard such people referred to as 'workhorses.'"

"Workhorses! Tell me the truth, Jack. Is that how Bill sees me?"

"Well, listen to the description of all five levels and tell me where you see yourself and where you want to be. Okay?"

"Okay, but I think I'm getting sick to my stomach."

"You're fine and I'm oversimplifying. None of what I'm describing is fatal, and it needn't be permanent. *Now the fifth level is made up of those who link their own success to the prosperity of the enterprise.* Because they are committed, they focus their skills and abilities on what the organization is trying to achieve. They have a broad perspective on how and why the business operates the way it does, and they don't adopt an adversarial point of view. That attitude enables them to make a more effective contribution. *The organization usually puts its highest value on this level of commitment.*"

"So what you're saying is, so much of how you're seen by others is based on your attitude."

"That is what I'm saying, Sandra. Our attitudes show up in our behavior. In the end, that affects the way the organization views us and the way it rewards us."

"Okay. I'm in the workhorse group. Right?"

"What do you think?"

"I don't like it, but it's pretty accurate. So how do I break out of it and move to the fifth level?"

"Well, Bill has given you some hints. The plan you devise should take them into account. Volunteer for something, but be sure it gets you out of your office. There are always task forces and projects coming up."

"Yes, and I think Bill's looking for someone to coordinate the blood drive. I'm the woman for that. I usually donate anyway and I think it's worthwhile."

"That's a start, Sandra. You need to get out and around. Create opportunities for face-to-face contacts with people -- the sooner, the better. Read the annual and quarterly reports from cover to cover. Go to meetings. Get acquainted with people who've been around for a time. Ask good questions, and make notes of the answers. Oh, and make sure Bill is aware of what you're doing."

"How do I fit all that in when I'm already bringing work home?"

"The secret is to create discretionary time."

"Discretionary time? I'm overbooked right now. How do you do it?"

"Sandra, the way I do it may not work for you."

"Come on, Jack. Give to the poor."

"You're not poor, but here goes. Let's get back to Sandra, Inc. She has a *role* to perform -- notice, I didn't say a *job*. So, the first thing is to clarify your role with Bill, one more time. Why does PWE have someone doing what you do? What value does the role have? Next, look at the work. Does it all make sense given your role? If not, separate those items that contribute from those that merely use up time. Pick out what you can stop doing, and stop doing it. Put the rest in priority order. And don't forget to talk to your other customers too, those you interact with and who use your work product. None of us work in a vacuum. For some people, you are a supplier of services; for others, a customer. Those people in the process know what part of your work adds the most value and the least. Get them to tell you. That can be very convincing information in talking with Bill. And don't forget to ask for some personal feedback from them as well. It's all good information for Sandra, Inc."

"Okay, I get it. I'm going to develop a plan -- and run it by Bill. That's after I've gone over it with you, if you're willing."

"Of course, I'm willing. Aren't you going to read every page of my book and talk it over with me? That's reciprocity, my friend. You said there was a second piece in the story that had a special message. What was it?"

"It was when the Elder asked Keli what he wanted and then what he had given to make it happen. Jack, I took a deep breath before I read on."

"Why is that?"

"Because I can see that I have been sitting in my office waiting for good things to happen. No wonder they haven't."

"But you're going to make them happen, Sandra. That's what it's all about. Let's talk about Bill's other comment, the one where he told you to 'lighten up.' What's that about? Do you think it was a general comment or specific to the occasion?"

"Both, I think. He told me that I seem to require a lot of positive support and praise, as if I constantly have my hand out. He says that when he gives me feedback about ways I can improve that I get defensive. I admit I can be oversensitive, but -- is that the way I come across to you, Jack?"

"To be honest, it isn't. But what we are talking about is not fact but perception. It's the way Bill experiences you. The question isn't who is right or wrong, but rather how you can change Bill's perception and let him see the Sandra I see. Let's talk about a plan."

"I think I need to meet with him, don't you?"

"I do. You need to get more information. But don't walk into his office without a plan. *The secret is, enlist his support. Make him a co-conspirator in your success and you're a shoo-in.* Also, that will help him see you as more willing to accept feedback. It's a good start at mending fences."

"So you don't think I'm hopeless."

Jack smiled. "Not completely," he said.

Sandra laughed. "Thanks a lot, Jack. You're a big help. Anyway, I'm going to work on my plan this afternoon, and I'll read the rest of Chapter Two tonight. If you're free for a few minutes after lunch tomorrow, I'd like to stop by and discuss both of them."

They agreed on two o'clock the following day. Steve had returned from the trip with work to do, so Sandra curled up on the sofa and continued reading.

It was three days before I spoke more than a few words to the Elder. I had been busy due to his efforts on my behalf. True to his word, he had given my name to Bari, the Hunter, who was in charge of the celebration, and I was soon engaged in small tasks like gathering sticks of wood for the cooking fire and flowers to decorate the Tribal Chief's house. I'm not sure, but I think Bari was testing my resolve by assigning me these small tasks, for the next day he sent Pardo, the Trader, to ask me to help plan the dancing. This was much more to my liking since it involved talking to villagers who had only nodded to me in passing before. Because I was eager to help, Pardo, Bari and the others relied on me, and I did all they asked and more.

The night of the celebration, I stood watching as the dancers performed. They had dances about almost every aspect of village life, but I particularly enjoyed the one about the hunt. The dancers wore extra layers of beads around their necks, wrists and ankles. Their bodies were heavily painted with pictures and symbols of animals. Some of the dancers played the role of the hunters while others pretended to be jaguars, caimans, pythons and tapirs.

There were other dances too, some that told the history of the tribe and one that told about headhunters and tribal wars fought many years ago. All were dedicated to our Tribal Chief in whose honor we celebrated. We feasted on tapir meat and smoked fish. Roasted yams abounded. I was proud because I had a part in it, no matter how small. Maybe next time I would have even a greater role.

Many of the villagers came and sat beside me for a few minutes that night to pass the time. Several of the older ones remembered my mother and were grieved to learn of her death. It was strange. I had been in the tribe two years, but this was the first time I had felt a part of it. There was a hand on my shoulder, a familiar callused hand. "My young friend, many seek your company tonight."

Before I could jump up, he sat down cross-legged beside me. "Father, this has been the best three days since I came to the tribe. And I have you to thank for it."

"Not so, Keli, for my part in it was very small," said the Elder.

"But I would never have had this evening if you hadn't talked to Bari and Pardo."

"Nor would you have had this evening if you had not talked about your dreams. *For no one can guess at what another needs.*"

"It's just that I never felt anyone cared enough."

"Never forget, Keli, all things lie in wait for those who would reach out their hands to another."

*   *   *

"You do like my plan, don't you Jack?" asked Sandra putting her papers back in her briefcase.

"I do," he replied. "I think it addresses Bill's concerns and at the same time gets you started on your strategy to get out of the office, meet more people and broaden your interests. I think Bill will also be impressed with the thought you've given to your role. Once you both agree, things will start happening."

"Well, I'm going to acknowledge right up front that I need his advice and his help."

"Nice work, Sandra."

"The story -- I like the way the chapter ended. I can identify with Keli, I mean when he doesn't ask for what he wants. Sometimes, I don't either. That always feels so risky. It's easier to stay in your shell."

"It is. But when you stay in your shell, no one can help you, and you stand no chance at all of getting what you want. Let me tell you a quick story, Sandra. Several years ago there was a shortage of available computers at PWE. At the time, I was supervising a group of people writing press releases and news items. Well, we added a person to the group, but we were short one computer. Then I learned of one that was sitting in a vacant office. I went to my supervisor and told her I wanted to take that computer and give it to Mary Ellen. I explained to her that it was an important work tool for someone who would do a lot of writing and revisions. She agreed and the computer was delivered. About a week later, Jerry Evans came to me and said, 'How did you get that computer? I had my eye on it.' 'I asked for it,' I replied. 'I understand it's been in that vacant office for the last two months.' 'I know,' said Jerry. 'but I was waiting for Christine to come around and ask who needed it.' Now eventually Jerry got a computer, but I never felt bad for taking that one. That's one of the secrets of the jungle. *If you want to get what you need, you have to ask.*"

"But what if you are told 'no.'"

"Sandra, *one of the ways we can all 'lighten up' and I'll include myself in this, is to learn how to hear things we don't want to hear. That includes feedback, and it includes 'no.'* Most of my supervisors were willing to explain when they told me 'no.' More often than not I hadn't been totally clear about why I was making the request or how others would benefit. Many times I was able to win a concession to come back with more information and ask again later. *The secret is the more we listen, the more we understand; and the more we understand, the stronger and more capable we become.*"

"Jack, I had one more question. Several times in the story you mention the word *path*. What is it and are you going to talk some more about it?"

"It's a career path, jungle version. I'm in the midst of writing Chapter Three right now, and I can guarantee you'll hear a lot more about it in there."

"I can hardly wait," she grinned.

Back in her office a few minutes later, Sandra took out her journal and wrote:

Sandra's Journal

The Second Lesson

To survive, think of yourself as a business -- like Sandra, Inc.
To succeed, ask for what you need, including information about
*   how you are perceived.*
The secret is, people can and do make different commitments, but
*   the greatest rewards come to those who link their success with*
*   the success of the enterprise.*

> "Attempt the end, and never stand to
> doubt;
> Nothing's so hard but search will find
> it out."
> ...Robert Herrick

THE THIRD LESSON

On Making Career Decisions

It was several months later when Sandra came to Jack for advice. Things were going better for her at PWE. In fact, she had been offered a transfer to the Marketing Department, and she wasn't sure whether to take it.

"I don't know what to do," she said. "This is in Sales and I've never done it before. I'm not sure I'd like it. And I don't know anything about the Marketing Department. Bill thinks I should take it. He told me he would hate to lose me, but it's a great opportunity. Tell me what to do. I really trust your judgment."

Jack smiled. "I'm happy for you. It's great to have choices. I'd be glad to help you explore them, but you have to make the decision. Finding the path is important work," he continued. "It's too important to trust to anyone else. Tell you what, why don't you read the next chapter of the book, think about it, and we'll talk tomorrow."

Sandra agreed. That night she read the third chapter.

The Four Paths

I was ready to explore the jungle, but which of all the possible paths should I take? I wasn't sure what I was looking for: only that it was time to begin the search. I needed some advice. I found the Elder as he was leaving a tribal council. He beckoned to me and we sat on a fallen tree limb by the edge of the pond. For the first few moments we enjoyed the stillness together. Then I asked for his help.

"There are many paths through the jungle," he said. "Tomorrow, we will walk the path that leads to the tallest mountain."

We began our walk early the next morning. As we left the village, the Elder pointed out subtle changes in the terrain. Near the village was a quiet stream, but as we walked further toward the mountain, the current began to move faster and faster. In areas where the river expanded, the dense growth of vines, small trees and shrubs made walking difficult. The higher altitude left me short of breath.

We had gathered some berries as we walked along the path, and we stopped for lunch in a small clearing. "I never realized how much is required on the path to the mountain." I observed.

The Elder nodded. "You must be totally committed if you choose this path. Many start up the path and change their minds along the way."

"Why?" I wondered.

"As we walk higher and higher you will find the path more narrow and fallen trees along the way that form natural barriers. It is a hard path, and it requires many sacrifices. Much of the excitement of the mountain is in the challenges you must overcome. The rewards are great. Would you like to continue?"

I thought for a few minutes. The Elder was silent. What intrigued me about the mountain was the view I would see as I moved higher. There would be a feeling of power as I looked down toward the village. But I wasn't sure those were the rewards that would satisfy me the most. I told the Elder I wanted to explore some of the other paths before I decided.

He agreed and we met the next morning to talk about the other paths and decide which of them to try.

This time we headed down a more quiet path, away from the river's edge. The Elder led silently, and I, unsure of our destination, walked briskly behind. Finally, we came to the foot of a small hill. A narrow stream ran along the side and we stopped for a refreshing drink. "Where are we going?" I asked. The Elder pointed toward the top and we continued our journey. The trees in this area of the jungle were smaller and closer together, but the path was more defined and easier to travel than the one we had taken the day before.

When we reached the top, The Elder used a small branch to draw four lines in the dirt. "These are the paths open to you," he said, pointing to the lines. "This path goes through the wildest part of the jungle. It is the path of the Hunter. Of all people in the tribe, the Hunter is the most valued, for he brings home the tapir meat and peccary skins that enable the tribe to survive. His is the most exciting work -- and the most dangerous."

"Look there," he said, and I saw a path that was heavily covered with undergrowth, tangled thickets and climbing palms. It looked at once challenging and forbidding. "If you take this path, you will go with others into places no one has been before, and test your skills against jaguars and caimans, in forests where bushmasters lie in wait and rivers are filled with piranha. If you are successful, you will return as a hero. It is the path of adventure, and those who take it must learn to be expert with blowguns, arrows and machetes. They must also be brave. In our tribe, it is usually those hunters who have survived the greatest dangers who are chosen to go to the top of the tall mountain."

"The second path is that of the Toolmaker," he continued, pointing to a path leading from the village to another clearing. "This is the path of the craftsman. To follow it you must learn to shape bows and carve arrows from the purple wood of the spotted snakewood tree and turn the peccary and capybara skins brought back by the Hunters into leather goods that the tribe can trade for supplies."

"Peccary? What are they?" I asked.

"You may know them as water hogs," he replied. "They are an excellent source of leather and meat as are the capybara."

"Aren't they rodents?" I asked.

"Very large ones. They make the best leather for their skins are thick and soft. If you would be successful as a Toolmaker, you must not only know your craft but be constantly looking for ways to make better bows and finer leathers at the same time you reduce what must be thrown away. We Korios place a high value on nature's gifts and we do not sacrifice any of them without respect. Those who take this path must be creative and take great pride in the work of their hands."

Motioning me to turn in a new direction, the Elder pointed toward the river. "That is the path of the Trader," he said. I saw where the river forked away from the mountain and toward another part of the jungle. "The Trader must know the value of the different skins and tools we make as well as the supplies we are trading for. He must have the skills to bargain with those who would buy our products for too little and sell theirs for too much. He must know the moment when the trade should be made."

"It sounds like Traders have to think fast and be good talkers."

"Yes. To walk any path, you must use your intelligence and reasoning skills, but the Traders must use their minds and voices like the craftsman uses his tools."

"Do they climb the tall mountain?"

"Some do. Most set their sights on one of the other mountains, not as tall but just as challenging."

We turned once more, and I saw a small group of people walking along a path carrying baskets full of foliage. "They are the Healers," said the Elder. "Those roots, berries and leaves they carry make medicines and balms with curative power. The Healers are knowledgeable about many areas that apply to people, and the villagers depend upon them for advice and counsel in every aspect of their lives. They travel the fourth path you may take," he said pointing to a dense area overgrown with shrubs, vines, and small trees."

"And do they climb the tall mountain?"

"If you choose the path of the Healer, you may not climb that mountain, but you will be a valued counselor to those who do. There are other mountains you can climb, if you choose to."

Just then I noticed another group of villagers. Unlike the other groups, they did not appear to be walking on a path but rather ambling around the clearing. Every few minutes, one or two broke away and wandered toward one of the four paths. The others laughed and pointed at the wanderers who soon returned to the group shaking their heads and shrugging their shoulders.

In a minute, several others began walking from path to path. As I watched, one or two disappeared down one path only to retrace their steps and head for a second path. I was confused. "What are they doing?"

"They have not yet found their purpose," he explained. "They cannot decide which path to take because they do not know what they want."

"But what will happen to them?" I wondered.

"Most will choose the path that leads to contentment. A few will choose the path that leads to dissatisfaction. A third group will not choose at all but continue to float from path to path. They are the Drifters."

"Drifters? What do they do?"

"They live their lives without purpose or commitment. If someone asks them, 'What do you want?' they shrug their shoulders and walk away. If someone says, 'Make a choice,' they say, 'It doesn't matter.' *Do not travel the way of the Drifter for it is the path of purposelessness and it leads to unhappiness.*"

"Which of the paths should I take?"

"Do you wish to climb the tall mountain?"

"I might want to climb one of the others but not the tall one. The road is too hard. I'm not an adventurer either, and while I think the way of the Hunter is exciting, I'm sure it is not for me. I am not sure whether I want to be a Trader or a Healer."

"It is good for you to make this decision now, for the tall mountain is challenging, and those who would climb it must not only be dedicated but must make the decision early."

And so we talked for a long time. The Elder encouraged me to choose the work I would find most fulfilling. He asked me many questions about the things I had enjoyed doing in the past and what my reasons might be for choosing either path. I finally decided I needed to continue exploring. I would go to each group and learn more about what it did. That decided, I was still worried. What if I made the wrong choice?

The Elder thought for a moment. Then he said, "*Those who are wise consider the way out as they seek the way in.* When you go to the Traders, you must talk to Talu. He is an Elder who sits close to the Chief Trader and will make a valuable friend. I will help you with the Healers. Once you have chosen your path, work diligently to learn all there is for you to know. Do more than is expected, for that is the way to growth. Look upon each task not as work but as an opportunity to build your skills. When you have done all these things, you will have proven yourself. Then, if you discover you have chosen a path that is not rewarding, we will support your making a change."

I felt better. There was a lot to think about in choosing a path, but I now understood that I really had more choices and more control than I had formerly believed.

Sandra put the manuscript on Jack's desk. "I liked this part. It gave me something to think about. I don't want to 'climb to the top of the mountain' either, but I wouldn't mind the view from part way up. I think I'll take the suggestion of the Elder and talk to the Marketing Department. If it works out, I'll take that job. If I'm not happy, I'll come back here. I really enjoy the work we're doing."

"I don't want to leave you with the impression that you should 'try it out,'" said Jack. *"There are many ways to transform a job you don't enjoy into one you do.* I remember one job I had. It was one-third selling, one-third reporting, and one-third handling all the customer complaints. I found that I really enjoyed the selling, found the reporting dull, and disliked handling everyone's problems. The first six months of that job I reduced the amount of reporting by over half."

"How did you do that?"

"I examined the reports and determined how much each one cost PWE. I asked the people who received the report how it was used. I found some reports were filed, but not used. Some were used partially, and some were used for making key decisions. Because I was able to show how much they cost, I had no arguments from anyone when I stopped doing the ones that weren't used. I redesigned those that were partially used, in most cases combining them and making them shorter and, in some cases, adding the information to the reports that were used. By the way, Sandra, that's one of my best-kept secrets. *Always know what the work you do costs.* At PWE it's a compelling reason for not doing things that don't benefit the company."

"What did you do with the extra time? Did you handle more complaints? Or did you do more selling?"

"My second goal was to reduce the time I spent handling customer complaints. Let me be clear. I never minded handling any complaints from my customers. Complaints help us be more effective, and I got larger sales and more loyalty from those customers who were willing to complain than from those who wouldn't. What I didn't like was handling everyone's complaints. That was always the work given to the newest employee."

"But I had a plan. What I did was to calculate the value of my customer complaints, and show the percentage of sales increases I had gotten from them to PWE's advantage. I took this information to my boss who asked me to make a presentation to the whole group. Once everyone had this information, there was a mob scene at my office with each salesperson eager to retrieve the complaints that belonged to him. It turned out to be a great sales tool, and my boss commended me for it. It was at this point that I learned another secret of the jungle. *Along with knowing the cost of the work you do, it is important to know the value, in real money.* Before long, I was spending about two-thirds of my time selling with one third split between complaints and reports, and I really loved that job."

"Did you ever have a job you just hated?"

"I did have one that I didn't enjoy. In fact, it was the one before my selling job. It was described to me as a coordinator's job, but I soon learned that it was shuffling lots of paper. The job was a series of activities and few of them were profitable. I was working with outside companies that were supposed to locate materials we needed. I had to keep extensive records, respond to inquiries from other companies that wanted to supply the materials, and keep them from hounding our manager. My phone rang all day long from outside salespeople trying to sell their products, and I took my briefcase home every night bulging with paperwork."

"The funny part of it is, the Engineering and Manufacturing Departments did not need or want the work I was doing because they had their own suppliers. What's more, they resented all the reports they had to submit to me. Consequently, I had to cajole them every month to submit the numbers I needed for my report. *You know, Sandra, one thing I view as fundamental to success -- and that is understanding how the work we do fits in and contributes to a whole process.* The more I looked at this job, the more I realized, it wasn't part of the process at all -- just an added step that created waste for others, and they let me know it."

"Whew! That sounds like the job from hell!"

"It was. I did reorganize it and I put what I could on a computer. I also ran some supplier surveys to see how we could improve the process from our end. I taught my secretary how to screen the calls. While I usually don't like to do that, I had to if I was going to get anything done. In the end, I plotted my escape."

"I must know -- how did you do it?"

"I took advantage of an opportunity. Mary had been on a committee to determine what kind of customer and supplier surveys were needed in their organization. The person in Marketing who was their resident expert on surveys was transferred. Mary knew I was the only one around who had experience with surveys of that size. She suggested the committee ask for my help. Before long, I was an advisor to their committee. Soon after that Marketing arranged a transfer and I wound up in the Sales job."

"Was Mary your supervisor?" asked Sandra.

"Nope," replied Jack. "I never worked for her -- just with her."

"Sounds like it was a combination of mentoring and opportunity that helped you make your escape from that awful job."

"It was more than that, Sandra. Mentoring played a key role, but I was ready. Albert Einstein put it best when he said, 'Chance favors the prepared mind.' *One of the rules of the jungle is to continuously expand your capabilities. The more you can contribute, the more likely the right opportunities will show up.*"

Sandra nodded. "I've been to several really good training classes."

"The right training can help a lot, Sandra, because it can give you the principles and the practice. But you grow most from doing the work itself. *Take on projects that give you the opportunity to learn. You just have to keep stretching yourself.*"

The meeting ended abruptly when Bill's secretary arrived with a message for Sandra. He was waiting and needed to see her right away.

The next morning Sandra left Jack a note saying she needed to talk about her meeting with Bill. Several hours later, they were huddled in Jack's office. "What's up?" he asked.

"I went to Marketing, and I like the job. I told Bill I wanted to take it. Then, out of the blue, he said he wanted me to think about it. He said I was just hitting my stride here. He started singing my praises, telling me how important I was to the group and suggesting that I would probably not be happy in that job. Now, I don't know what to do. Jack, I'm torn. I didn't sleep at all last night."

"You said you wanted the sales job."

"I do -- but it's so tempting to stay here and enjoy all the appreciation I'm getting. I thought I was stuck. Now I'm wondering if I am walking down the right path by leaving."

Jack nodded sympathetically. "As I said before, the choice of paths is yours, not mine and not Bill's. Can I tell you about a similar experience I had? It was in the Sales job I enjoyed so much. In fact, there were moments when I was sure I should never leave it. I had become expert at what I did. My name echoed through the halls. 'Ask Jack.' 'Jack can tell you.' 'Don't do it unless you talk to Jack first.' It was very seductive. I was having a great time. My boss trusted my judgment. He was always confiding in me."

"I had been in that job close to five years. One day the boss called me into his office. He had been scheduled to make a presentation to the whole Marketing Department, but he had to change his plans. The presentation was the next day, and he wanted me to give it in his place. I had done most of the work for it, so I was familiar with all the material. After my part of the program, several of the managers told me how good it was and two of them asked me where my boss had been hiding me."

"Several days later my boss came to my office and closed the door. He said, 'Jack, I've got to tell you, you did such a fine job on that presentation that one of the other managers offered a transfer. Are you interested?'"

"I thought about it for a few minutes and told him I was. He looked crestfallen. 'I was hoping you wouldn't be. I really need you here,' he said. 'We make a great team. I depend on you.' I was flattered, but the more I thought about it, the more I thought the offer was worth considering. It turned out to be a promotion, but even if it hadn't been I knew I should take it. I was getting stale. *I learned two important secrets from that experience: First, don't be seduced by your own importance or by the need to have others singing your praises. Second, don't be impossible to replace.* In fact, I'd go a step further. *You can help yourself and the organization at the same time by actively finding and coaching your replacement.* That way, you can continue to grow and go on to something even more exciting."

Sandra looked relieved. "Thanks, Bill. I knew you could help. I was falling into the same situation you were in. Now I know what to do."

"Be kind to Bill. He'll miss you. So will I."

"Jack, you won't have time to miss me. I look to you for guidance, and as a good friend. In fact, have you finished the next chapter of the book? If so, I'd love to read it."

Reaching in his desk, Jack pulled out the manuscript. Grinning, he handed Sandra a copy. "I thought you'd never ask," he said.

Picking up her briefcase, Sandra walked toward the door. Then she paused. "Jack, I have something I want you to look at. I'm keeping a journal to capture the main ideas. Let me show you what I wrote for Chapter Three."

Intrigued, he opened the journal and read the entry. "I like it!" he said.

Sandra's Journal

The Third Lesson

To survive, focus on adding value in every role.
To succeed, choose the work you find most fulfilling.
The secret is, use your work to build your capabilities. The more
*   you contribute, the more opportunities will show up.*

> "Each friend represents a world in us,
> a world possibly not born until they
> arrive,
> and it is only by this meeting that a
> new world is born."
> ...Anäis Nin

THE FOURTH LESSON

On Teams, Relationships and Networks

Between job changes and office moves, almost four weeks passed before Sandra was able to find a quiet evening to read the next chapter. Jack had called to see how things were going with Sandra's new position in Marketing, and she had invited him to stop by to see her in the morning. That night, with the manuscript in hand, Sandra stretched out on the sofa and began reading.

The Team

I had chosen the path of the Healer. The Elder was very pleased with my decision because he too was a Healer. He took me to the Wiseman, who represented the Healers on the Tribal Council. The Wiseman welcomed me into the group and introduced me to Mali, one of the Sorters, who was to be my teacher. I was assigned to a small group sorting leaves, roots and berries. My job was to take the baskets loaded with the different kinds of vegetation which had been collected by the Gatherers and separate the contents by type. When I completed a basketful, I was to take the piles to a second group of Sorters to be further divided based on how they would be prepared. Some would be used as balms to be applied directly to wounds or insect bites; some, as medications to be taken by mouth; others, as rubs for aches and pains.

I caught on quickly and was soon happily at work. What I enjoyed most was learning the names of the different types of leaves, feeling their texture, and comparing them with one another. I soon learned the names of the berries, tasting each type and finding some of them quite delicious, while others were strong and unpleasant. I did not taste the roots for I had been warned that some of them were poisonous.

When I completed my work, I watched a group of Healers who were preparing medications. Some were puncturing the bark from a brownish, gray tree to extract copal. Others were grinding leaves of the konoya plant to make tea for treating colds and sore throat. One was splitting the green nuts of the cashew tree to make a balm that would kill botfly larva lodging in the skin. This work looked more interesting to me than sorting, so I went to Mali. "I don't like sorting anymore," I said. "It's too menial. I want to work with the Medicine Makers."

Mali smiled. "You have much to discover where you are, Keli. There are many more roots, berries, flowers, shrubs than the ones you have worked with. Be patient. Pay attention to details, and learn from those around you. When you have proven yourself as a Sorter, you will be given other, more difficult work to do."

Several days later, I noticed that Manu, a Sorter who worked with me and was usually friendly, did not respond when I greeted him. At first, I thought he had not heard me, but when I repeated the greeting, he shrugged and walked away. Later that day I saw him talking to Mali and nodding in my direction. Then he whispered something to Tari, another Sorter who worked with us. That evening, I asked Tari if she knew what was wrong. She responded, "Manu saw you helping Koita split the cashew nuts. He felt you should have asked if one of the Sorters needed you before you went to the Medicine Makers and helped them."

I was puzzled by these events and decided to get Mali's opinion. She listened and nodded as I told my story. "You are very bright," she told me, "and you are quick to learn. In time you will be one of the best Healers we have. You have asked for my counsel, so think of this: those who work beside you may also need your help. Do not forget to join hands with them, lest they see you as an outsider."

Early the next morning, Jack stopped by Sandra's office. "What did you think of Chapter 4?" he asked.

"I haven't finished it. I am interested in why you started the chapter on the tribe by talking about teamwork."

"Because I believe that *you cannot be a star until you've recognized the importance of being a team member.* Sandra, have you ever watched a winning basketball team. A great player who is not a team member can still shoot many baskets, but it's no guarantee the team will win. A great player who is a team member, however, raises the standard and quality of play for everyone. I believe it's the same way in business. We all need each other. The secret is to *stay aware of the impact of our actions on those around us.*"

"Manu was angry with Keli for two reasons: first, because he didn't treat the team as important when he went to help the other group before the team had completed all the baskets; and second, because he violated a norm. Violating a rule can get you in trouble with your boss, but violating a norm hurts you with your team."

"I know what a norm is," said Sandra. "It's an unspoken rule in a work group. It's eating lunch together on a Friday, or taking turns doing some of the less pleasant work or helping your own team first. I think Manu was childish by the way he handled the situation. I would have told Keli about it rather than whispering to Tari and Mali."

"That's for sure. He probably violated a norm as well. And he clearly didn't understand one of the secrets: *never go to your supervisor and complain about another member of the team unless it's about something very serious. It makes you look powerless.* The thing that works in Manu's favor is that he clearly has been there longer than Keli so the team recognizes his value. Now it's Keli's responsibility to earn his place on the team."

"I wonder how Keli and Manu are going to mend their relationship in the story."

"I guess you'll have to keep reading," said Jack. But enough of the jungle for now. How are things going in the new sales position?"

"Great, I guess. I do have one concern. Every time I send Karen a report, letter or E-mail document, she thanks me for the information and attaches a question, note, or suggestion for follow-up. It's getting to the point where I don't like to send her notes. Most of the questions or suggestions are time killers, and they really don't add value. I know details are important, but I don't know how much time or effort to give the notes. Help!"

"Have you discussed it with her?"

"She says everything is important -- that she likes to keep on top of things. One of the other salesmen tells me she compares her style to that of a helicopter hovering over the action."

Jack laughed. "Sounds like she may land a bit too often. At any rate, Sandra, it is having an impact on you. I'll tell you how I have handled that situation in the past, but I'll add one caution. First of all, the method. Begin by dividing the notes into categories. The first category is of good ideas, ones that you want to follow up on. Do those. The second is of things that you know are important to Karen. Usually you can tell by phrases like 'get back to me on this' or expressions like *ASAP* (as soon as possible). Do those too."

"Then designate a drawer or a file for the ones that are suggestions. Date them and see if Karen remembers them. My bosses rarely did. Their scribbles on my reports or E-mail notes were passing thoughts. If she comments a second time, you may need to follow up. If it takes a lot of your valuable time, I'd talk with her first. *Don't be afraid to suggest an alternative. Remember, the more time you spend on inconsequential things, the less time you have to do what's important.*"

"Ninety-nine percent of the time this works. But be careful. If you're not alert to what's going on, there could be a problem. I remember one time when we received an angry letter from a company we no longer used as a supplier. It was from their marketing vice president who added that he planned to call our president. My boss had jotted a note on it and told me to 'put out this fire.' The key word was *fire* but I guess I wasn't paying attention. I spent some time researching the situation and wrote the marketing vice president a very good letter explaining our position, but it arrived too late. The marketing vice president made the call, and even though he never reached the president, my boss was extremely displeased and he let me know it."

"What could you have done?"

"I guess I could have gone right back to my boss and told him what I planned to do. That would have given him more options. He thought I should have called the man, but I didn't think a phone call from me would have done anything more than fan the flames."

"I don't think it was fair for him to blame you. He was asking you to do the impossible."

"Maybe it wasn't fair, but I learned a long time ago if you spend your time worrying about making everything fair, you waste time and energy. The important thing is what I learned from it."

"What's that?"

"Sometimes the things that appear the least important to you can be the most important to someone else. So what I'm telling you is read the signals. Begin to listen to Karen so you can tell the difference between what is important and what's interesting, between a request and a suggestion. I failed to give it the proper importance because it wasn't important to me, and it was reflected in my performance review that year."

"But couldn't you have complained about that to the manager?"

"I never considered it. It's an unwritten rule in any company that *people who complain get tagged as complainers.* That puts everyone in a difficult position: you, the boss, and the manager. I would make one exception to that rule: if you were asked to do something illegal, immoral, or unethical. Then you have no choice."

"Has anyone…?"

Jack shook his head. "Never. I think the managers at PWE are decent and honest people. I may not agree with them all the time, but that's the jungle, isn't it."

Sandra smiled. In parting, she promised to get back with Jack in two or three days to discuss Chapter 4. She was eager to read how Keli and Manu worked out their differences. That night, she picked up the manuscript and continued the story.

I was perturbed about the situation with Manu for several reasons. First, I could see that the problems between us were affecting the whole group. Second, it was hard to solve a problem with someone who refused to speak. I felt Manu was being unreasonable and stubborn. When I approached Tari to ask for her advice, she suggested I talk to Pola, a Senior Healer, who was much in demand for the quality of advice she gave the villagers on all sorts of matters regarding their work, their health, and their relationships. Pola agreed to help.

That afternoon Pola, Manu and I met at the pond. Pola talked for a few minutes about finding a solution that would be good for both Manu and me. She asked each of us to describe what happened while the other listened without speaking. We were allowed to ask each other questions, but we couldn't interrupt or contradict the other. That was hard. Then Pola asked us each to say one thing we valued about the other. I told Manu I liked the way he was willing to share secrets that made the work go faster. Manu said he appreciated the way I listened and asked questions. After that each of us described one thing the other could do to make our working relationship better. That was easy. Manu wanted me to help the team first. I nodded eagerly. I wanted Manu to tell me directly if I bungled again. Manu looked down for a moment, and then extended his hands in a gesture of apology. I extended mine as well. Pola smiled. "I think this is a good first step," she said. "Now, you must agree when you will meet and check to be sure things are working better for you."

After that episode, we met a number of times at the end of our evening meal and walked by the river. With each successive meeting, we became more open in discussing how things were going between us. After a while, when our evening discussions began to cover a much broader range of topics, Pola and Mali asked if they could walk along with us. Then I felt like a true member of the team.

In fact, we became so close that I was really heartsick to learn that Manu was moving to a Healer Gatherers' group in a small village miles away. We agreed to send messages by runners moving between those areas. The morning he was leaving, Manu took Pola, Mali and me to the clearing and with a narrow stick drew a simple map to show us how to get to the village. We embraced and agreed to visit each other often.

"I like the way that turned out," said Sandra. She was seated opposite Jack in the company cafeteria. "Now that Manu and Keli are separated, I wonder if they will keep in touch."

"Sure they will," said Jack. "And even though Keli is sad, he will probably soon realize the value Manu has as a member of his network."

"You've always had a great network, Jack. What do you use it for mostly?"

"Information, contacts, getting resources. If I have a project, and I want to know how others have used a product or who might give me some information about it, it helps to be able to ask someone. Often there's a chain. My source might not know, but be aware of someone who does. The answer is frequently a few phone calls away, but you have to know the right people to call."

"If I'm getting ready to go into a meeting and there are some people I don't know who will participate in making an important decision, I might get in touch with one of my network to find out how that person might respond."

"Perhaps I might want to meet someone in another department," continued Jack. "It helps to know someone who can pave the way.

Sometimes people in your network can help you when you just need someone to lend a hand. Often, they come up with an idea or another way of seeing things. One thing's for sure, my friends have come to my rescue more than once."

"Do you have a network outside the company too?"

"Yes. That's equally important. I remember when I was part of a team that did a benchmark study on marketing. Once we had decided which companies were the most outstanding in the area of marketing we were studying, we had to talk with the people from those companies who could help. Believe it or not, getting them to return our calls was the hardest part. Those people also have busy schedules, and they didn't know who we were. But, between my network and those of the others on the team, we were able to make the contacts we needed at every company we wanted to visit."

"How do you create a network?"

"Well, it's easier to do that within PWE than outside our company. *Inside, I make a point to be friendly with a lot of people.* There are many ways to meet people, Sandra. Consider everyone you meet as a potential addition to your network. Project teams and task forces are good sources. So are meetings. When you attend a meeting or go to training, sit with people you don't know and invite them to join you for lunch. They're always glad to have someone to talk to. Ask questions, listen and learn. Be willing to share information. Remember, the old concept of reciprocity. The principles of creating good relationships never change. *That requires genuine interest in others coupled with the willingness to go the extra mile for them.*"

"Above all, *don't rely exclusively on computers and telephones every time you need to contact people.* You'd be surprised how much easier it is to work through disagreements when you've met face to face. Computers and telephones are great tools, but they ought to carry a warning label: 'Caution: not the best way to build a network.' At the same time, they can be useful in sustaining a network. When you use these tools, don't forget the personal touch."

"But computers and telephones save a lot of time, don't you think?"

"They do. And I use them a lot, but it's very hard to convey personal warmth on them. No matter what methods you use, _communicate_. Don't forget, Sandra, _building a network is an important part of your job, and it's one of the secrets of the jungle._"

"So, how do you build an external network? Or more important, how did you build yours?"

"I belonged to professional organizations, and I went to meetings. I donated time to charitable organizations. They're a networking goldmine. Occasionally, I was able to attend an outside training program or a conference. I made an effort to meet as many people as I could. I talked to our suppliers in person. I met our customers. The more people you get to know, the better your network will be. One very important secret: _I learned people's names, and I made a point to remember them._"

"Oh, now you're into one of my biggest failings."

"Join the club. But there are books, audio tapes, and other training tools for people who know how important it is. Those are the ways I learned to do it. Even so, I try to make a few notes after I meet people for the first time. And I don't hesitate to ask someone to repeat a name if I didn't catch it. When I've done that, I've found people are relieved, and they usually ask me to repeat mine as well."

"So, the more activities I'm a part of, the more I'll build a network. Right?"

"Right. And that's one of the reasons I told you, long ago, that hard work is important, but it isn't enough. It's networks and mentors and building relationships across all sorts of boundaries that finally make a difference in your work-life experience. They are sources of light."

Sandra's Journal

The Fourth Lesson

To survive, differentiate between what is and is not important.
To succeed, be an active contributor to the team.
The secret is, develop ongoing relationships and networks.

> "In adversity, remember to keep an open mind."
> ...Virgil

THE FIFTH LESSON

On Choices, Pitfalls and Traps

Two taps on the door to Sandra's office. "Come on in," she said.

It opened. "Good morning. Hope I'm not interrupting," said Jack with a grin. "You've been hard to reach the last couple of weeks. I admit it, I'm checking up on you. Am I in the doghouse?" He paused and looked at her. "Where's that 'happy Sandra' look?"

"You know it's not you," said Sandra breaking into a smile. "Frankly, I should have stopped by to see you long ago. I've been on a project. Now it's 'down the tubes' and I hate to dump on you."

"I'm here now. Dump away."

"Please sit down, Jack. I may be in a bad mood, but I still have some manners left. Can I offer you coffee?"

He shook his head. "No coffee, thanks. I can tell, this is going to be a long story."

Sandra leaned forward. "I must admit, I'm feeling disgruntled - - and it is a long story. It all started a couple of weeks ago when Rich Cargell, Karen's boss, asked me to come by his office. He told me PWE was starting this year's Spirit of Volunteerism campaign. He told me all the usual stuff, 'good for community relations' 'great for morale,' you know what I mean."

Jack nodded. "It really is a worthwhile cause."

"I know," said Sandra. "Rich told me all the PWE business lines were represented on the committee and asked me to represent Marketing. He said the two previous campaigns really hadn't been all that exciting and management was looking for some sparkle. I can tell you honestly, Jack, I was flattered."

"That's quite a compliment, Sandra. And you're just the person to add that sparkle. So what happened?"

"Shortly after I met with Rich, I received a notice of the first committee meeting from Marjorie Anderson of Human Resources, the committee chairperson. I was really fired up by what Rich said and sure we could accomplish great things. Marjorie was very encouraging. 'No limits,' she said. By the second meeting, the committee had developed quite a list of recommendations. We thought of volunteering to teach a science class at the local high school and of offering a course on self esteem and positive thinking in the elementary and junior high schools to be taught by PWE volunteers. We thought about sponsoring a music and art festival, of taking on a particular charity and holding a benefit, of having a cleanup day in some area of the city, of sponsoring a debate or some other activity to increase understanding of local government -- you name it."

"Sounds like a very aggressive committee. What kind of support did you get for your ideas?"

"Well, Marjorie was enthusiastic. She thought all the ideas were wonderful, but she wanted to focus on the top three when she presented them to management. She asked us to flesh them out so they didn't seem 'off-the-wall.' Cindy and I took the one about sponsoring a music and art festival. To promote the idea, we went to a local chamber music group, and they agreed to put on a musical interlude in the cafeteria. We agreed on a Friday about one month later. That date is coming up next week. Cindy and I felt that would give us plenty of time to get approval and work the logistics. Then we visited three art galleries and got the owners to commit to thematic art shows in the lobby on three successive weeks. To top it off, we found two excellent speakers -- Estella Rivera, an expert in the music and art of the many cultures of our city, and Derek Townsend, a well known designer who could talk about our architectural history. We knew these activities would promote interest in the campaign and get volunteers for the festival."

"You went to a lot of work to put this together. How did Marjorie and the rest of the committee react?"

"Marjorie was ecstatic. Other members of the committee were impressed, but they were busy on the other two recommendations. We were all going like a house afire."

"I get the impression," said Jack softly, "that someone doused the flames."

Sandra nodded. "Last Friday I called Marjorie to find out who would be in charge of setting up the stage in the cafeteria for the chamber music this Friday. She hedged and stumbled around a bit, then asked me if I could come by her office. So I did. When I got there she told me she had finally met with the management group on Wednesday, and they had said the art could go on exhibit, but we could not have the chamber music in the cafeteria. They weren't sure we needed the speakers. I was stunned. I mean all of these people were donating their time in the interest of the community. This was just one week before the start-up date. When I asked her why, Marjorie said she thought management must have had a smaller plan in mind from the beginning. Jack, she never told any of us that. No limits! Then she said she had meant no limits on ideas. That's a cop out! She knew what we were doing. Cindy and I kept her informed from the start. We had been working on this for almost a month, and she didn't discuss our plans with the management group until last Wednesday when we'd already made the arrangements. All that work! All those commitments! I'm angry. She had two jobs to do -- and only two. To head the committee and to work with management. If she had done her job... Well, this wouldn't have happened."

"So, management did not want the music in the cafeteria. Did they object to having it somewhere else?"

"She said they would have to give it some consideration. We were placed in such a difficult situation. It was I who had begged these people to come, and now I may have to beg off. The other committee members ran into similar brick walls. We're all angry and disappointed. I must have gotten five calls since last Friday from people on the committee who wondered why we were bothering with this. My head is pounding, Jack. I don't know what to do."

"Sounds like you have three problems here: one, to find out what can be salvaged from the work you've already done; two, to mollify the people from the community who have made these commitments and may already have gone to some trouble to start fulfilling them; and three, to understand what management really had in mind so you can help the committee sort this out. Have I missed any?"

"Yes, Jack. There's one more. We are having a meeting tomorrow, and I'm wondering if I should nail Marjorie. She deserves it. What do you think?"

"Okay, let's take the Marjorie question first. We can talk about the other three problems later. If you're asking my advice, I'd say don't fall into the trap of talking to her when you're angry. And don't nail Marjorie in a meeting in front of everyone. What would that gain?"

"I might feel better, for one thing. Jack, she gave us bad signals and disrupted the work of everyone -- and I think she should know that."

"So do I, *but feedback like that is best given in private. Before you come down too hard, you probably want to give Marjorie a chance to explain what happened. Then, provide her with some information about the impact that her failing to get good information has had on you, the people in the community, and the other committee members.* Clearly, as the only committee member reporting to management, she had a responsibility -- and unless management gave her a surprise, she could have done a better job of handling it. Above all, remember, you might have to work with her again -- and chastising her in front of everyone won't help."

"You're right, but it'll be hard to back off. I mean, I've already let her know I'm not happy about the whole thing. What do I say to her that doesn't sound like I'm taking her on?"

"Use soft words, Sandra. Tell her you're puzzled by what happened and you'd like to understand. Tell her you're disappointed and you've been wondering what would have happened if she had met with management earlier. Words like that help set the stage for a discussion, not a scolding. They also put people in a problem solving mode. I'm not suggesting you let Sandra off the hook -- just that you don't say things you'll regret later."

"It always helps to talk to you. Do you have a chapter on situations like this one?"

"I do. Remember, early on in the book, the Elder warned Keli that those who didn't understand the jungle might be prey to its hidden dangers. I've written about some of these in the next chapter. If you want, I'll drop it by on my way to lunch."

"Thanks, Jack."

It was several hours later. Jack had dropped by briefly on his way to a meeting leaving the manuscript on Sandra's desk. Anticipating its arrival, Sandra had rushed down to the cafeteria where she had hastily grabbed a turkey sandwich and a soda and headed back to the office. Now, with lunch in front of her, Sandra settled back in her chair, kicked off her shoes and began Chapter 5.

Avoiding the Pitfalls

We had been walking along for about two hours now, searching for shemane fern. The Elder was ahead, and I walked behind for the path was narrow and overgrown. It was an oppressively hot morning, and the air was very still. The sky, what we could see of it through the dense canopy of trees, was overcast. Every now and then the Elder stopped to point something out to me -- a group of leafcutter ants carrying their spoils home, termites marching through the forest, a hummingbird vibrating red and green as it sipped nectar from the sweet flowers. We were looking for a place to rest when I came up to a small area where the growth was not as dense. I called to him and started to sit down, but he turned quickly and grabbed my arm. "Don't move!" he said.

I was startled. "Don't you wish to stop for a moment?" I asked.

"Not by this liana," he said, shaking his head. "It can give you a painful burn. That is why it is called a fireplant. You must be more careful, Keli. There are many dangers in the jungle for those who are not aware."

We continued walking for the next few minutes. Finally, we reached the river, and the Elder pointed to a fallen log several feet from its edge. "Let us sit here and watch the tall red birds catching fish." He smiled, "Perhaps we can learn how they do it."

We sat cross-legged side by side, leaning against the tree. "Father, have you heard what Pola has asked me to do?"

"I have. You are to go to the city with Pardo, the Trader, and Lutar, the Toolmaker, to buy clothing, blankets and other supplies for the Village. It is an honor to be chosen."

"Pola feels I know a lot about the city because I was raised there."

"That is only one of the reasons you have been chosen. You have shown a great willingness to help."

"I understand. Pola told me, but..."

"But?"

"But I have a problem, and I am not sure what to do. Pardo came to me the other night and told me he had been talking to several of the other traders. They think we should ask the villagers what other things they would like us to bring back."

"And?"

"Pardo has asked me to keep this from Lutar. He says because the Tool-maker is old and close to the Chief, he will not agree to this. I am in the middle and I don't know what to do."

"Whose mission is this?"

"Father, I have been told it is the Chief's mission."

"Who chose you for this mission?"

"Pola says it was the Shaman."

"What is the reason for the mission?"

"To buy the supplies needed for the tribe."

"Keli, suppose you go to the villagers. Each of them tells you what he or she wants. For Mali, it is a colorful skirt; for Bari, something to adorn his arrows; for little Tani, a special sweet. You make your list. Then you say, 'Give me something so I may pay for this in the city,' and each tells you, 'Go to the Chief and get something to trade.'"

"And the Chief, what would he do?"

"He would say, 'Why did you ask the villagers? For now, they are happy. Soon they will be disappointed.' So what would you say to that, Keli?"

"I don't know, Father."

"My son, there are many pitfalls in the jungle. You might trip over this log we're leaning against and fall into the river and drown or go fishing and step on the flat fish that stings. You understand these dangers. But there are other perils that lie in wait for the unwary. You must learn to see these too."

"What are they?"

"I cannot name them all, for it would be easy to forget some. But I will tell you what I can. One pitfall is following the way of Pardo instead of Lutar. Lutar knows why the Tribal Chief is sending you to the city. It is not to gratify the wishes of each of us as individuals but rather to supply the needs of the tribe as a whole. Pardo does not seem to understand this. So which should you follow?"

"Lutar."

"That is right. *For if you follow Pardo in this you would have been led in the wrong direction -- away from the real reason for your mission. And because you are a bright young man, you have also avoided the second pitfall -- acting in haste.* For when Pardo sought to include you in his plan, you did not rush to agree or disagree but rather stopped to think about it."

"But what if Pardo calls me 'coward'?"

"What if he does? It is not words but deeds that make one a coward. Act on what you know is true."

"Should I go to Lutar?"

"No. Just keep your own counsel. There will be other times when you and Pardo will see the same."

"Should I go to Pardo and tell him he should not have done this?"

"If you wish, my son. *But avoid the harshness of tone that comes from pronouncing yourself right and others wrong.* This too is a pitfall, for even though it may be true, it creates needless enemies. Always remember, next time you might be wrong."

"I will remember."

"*Do not be eager to assign blame for just as there is enough praise to go around, so the one who blames others will eventually find himself blamed.* These are the pitfalls of those too eager to act and too mindful of their own needs."

"Could one be overly cautious?" I wondered.

"Yes," said the Elder. "That is another pitfall, *for in our failure to act, decisions are made without us. Thus, we give up our freedom to choose. We must be thoughtful, but not afraid.*"

For a few minutes we sat in silence. Then my gaze was drawn to the river where two white herons emerged from behind the overhanging trees in search of fish. I walked to the water's edge. This was a part of the river I had never seen before. The water looked cool and inviting, but who could know if black caiman or flesh-eating fish lay beneath its surface.

As if he read my thoughts, the Elder spoke, "You have seen the tall birds fishing without fear. That is a good sign. Enjoy the river, Keli. Just be aware that it holds dangers as well as delights."

For a moment I stood there. Then I walked boldly in.

Jack picked up the telephone on the first ring. The caller ID said the voice on the other end of the line would be Sandra's. "Hi," he said. "I wasn't expecting to hear from you so soon."

The minute she responded he could tell things were better for her. "You sound like the old Sandra."

"Watch it. I'm not sure how I like your use of 'old' in front of my name. I finished the chapter during lunch, and I've had quite an afternoon. Do you have time to talk?"

Jack glanced at his watch. He had a meeting in ten minutes that promised to take the rest of the day. Tomorrow morning would be out as well because of Sandra's Volunteerism Committee meeting. They arranged to meet for coffee in Jack's office the following afternoon. "Actually, that'll work out fine," said Sandra, "because we can talk about the book, and I'll also be able to tell you about my conversation with Marjorie. By then the committee meeting will be history -- so you'll get a full report on that as well. I now have a plan --so keep your fingers crossed."

"Can I have a headline on the Marjorie talk? I hate to wait that long."

"Okay, Jack, here's your headline. 'Talks progressing between Sandra and Marjorie: Each side claiming victory.' Bye now."

He smiled and put down the phone. Rich was right. Sandra did sparkle.

* * *

It was just after two the next day. Jack was standing by the window, telephone to his ear as Sandra walked in his office. Motioning her to a chair, he took a deep breath and covered the receiver. "Won't be but a minute more," he promised.

Sandra looked at her watch as Jack hung up. "That was almost two minutes, but who's counting," she grinned.

"All right, mystery lady. The fun is over. I feel as if I'm in Part II or is it Part III of a Mini-Series. Tell me what's happened. The suspense is killing me."

"I think this is Part III with the end in sight. Yesterday, after you left and I read the chapter, I gave the situation some thought. There were certain things that stuck with me. The questions the Elder asked Keli about the purpose of the mission made me stop and think about what had happened in the committee. In some ways we got sidetracked by the desire to have everything complete and forgot to check back with management to see if we were heading in the right direction."

"That's an important lesson, Sandra. *It never hurts to try out your ideas before you get overinvested in them. And being clear about the purpose, scope and boundaries of any assignment is vital to its success and yours.* So what did you do?"

"Let me go through my thoughts first. If you hear the end of Part III too soon, you might decide to switch channels. Something you told me, perhaps in passing, made a lot of sense to me. Why not see what could be salvaged? So I sat down with Cindy and together we planned a strategy to use in talking with Marjorie. You had encouraged me to give Marjorie feedback in private, but Cindy and I were partners in this venture, so we decided to go in together."

"Good decision."

"I was also influenced by two other points in the story. The Elder tells Keli not to sound harsh -- and Cindy and I agreed with that. We were both nervous. In a way, going in to give Marjorie feedback was like when Keli walked into the river, feeling there might not be any crocodiles -- but you never know."

"So what happened?"

"Our strategy was a good one. First, we would offer Marjorie some helpful feedback. She needed to know how at least two members of the committee felt about what had happened in time to do something about it. When the project was over, it would be too late to make amends."

"How did that go?"

"Probably a little better than we thought it would. She wasn't eager to hear our thoughts, but once we got the discussion going, she admitted feeling that she had not done the proposal justice. We agreed with her -- but nicely, Jack."

"Good for you. I've seen more people try to take the sting out of feedback and spoil a good opportunity for growth on both sides. That's a way of treating people as if they are too weak to hear the truth and too powerless to change. I'm glad you didn't fall into that trap."

"Me too, but I must admit at one point it was tempting. I felt sorry for Marjorie, but she stood up pretty well considering she was 'outwomanned.' Once we had finished the feedback, we did get into some problem solving. Both Cindy and I agreed we might have gone overboard a bit, but our product was excellent for PWE and its Spirit of Volunteerism Campaign. In fact, we felt it important that in the name of good community relations, PWE welcome both of the speakers who are thought leaders in the community. Both had agreed to participate in the music and arts festival if management chose to sponsor it. Marjorie said she would take another stab at it, reminding management that backing off now could have a negative effect."

"Good thinking, Sandra. You and Cindy are a dynamite team."

She grinned. "As for the chamber music, we asked Marjorie why the objection to having it in the cafeteria. She said she would find out and call us back. At five o'clock I got a phone call from her. Cindy was rushing into my office, so I assumed correctly that Marjorie had called her first. Anyway, the latest is -- the speakers are back on, and they'll even be introduced by a member of the Management Council. How's that for a turn around? Management had not intended to have us cancel the chamber music -- only to move it from the cafeteria. They had felt it would be intrusive for the people eating there and impolite to the people playing. So I won't have to call them after all and tell them they've been canceled. They will play in the auditorium instead. Now, Cindy and I will have to do some real advertising to make sure people know. You've got to come, Jack. It's Friday from 11-12."

"I'll be there. Tell me, what will you write in your journal?"

"Here it is, Jack. Why don't you read it."

Sandra's Journal

The Fifth Lesson

To survive, understand the purpose, scope, and boundaries of every task.
To succeed, be honest without being harsh and courageous without being foolhardy.
The secret is, if you want to solve problems, avoid criticizing another in public or blaming another -- anywhere.

> "The choice of a point of view is the
> initial act of a culture."
> ...José Ortega y Gasset

THE SIXTH LESSON

On Handling Differences

"Getting back to the jungle, do you plan to write anything on the subject of turf situations?" asked Sandra. Boy, am I seeing those rise up in my new job."

"What's happening?"

"The problems are between headquarters and the field. The information flow is so poor that I've been asked to go out to one of our field locations and see if we can improve the situation. They have been dragging their feet about schedules. It's almost as if they're reluctant to have me come. Karen says that's typical."

"Looks like an opportunity to me."

"I'd like to think it is. It reminds me of some of the issues we used to have with Human Resources. Sometimes it feels as if we're more in competition with each other than with other companies."

"Sometimes we are. That's a great subject for..."

"Let me guess," said Sandra, extending her hand, palm upward, "it's Chapter 6."

He grinned. "You know me. And you're a great editor too. It's that reciprocity thing we talked about earlier."

The next three days were hectic for Sandra. After several meetings with Karen and numerous telephone calls, the trip had been expanded to three field locations. Between packing and several late meetings with Karen, she had no time to read the next chapter. Now wedged between two large people on a small turbo prop headed for Atlanta, she reached into her briefcase and pulled out the typewritten pages.

Resolving Conflicts

One morning just after sunrise the Shaman called all the Healers together. We gathered beside the hill to hear his words. Tomorrow, he told us, the Tribal Council would go to the mountain top to make plans for the months ahead. As Chief Healer, it was his responsibility to prepare the Healer Wiseman for this meeting. The Shaman asked us to meet within our four groups (Sorters, Gatherers, Medicine Makers and Counselors) sometime today to discuss anything we felt important for the Council to consider in developing the plan. At sunset one person from each of the four Healer groups would convey our ideas to the Shaman and the Elders. Those they deemed critical to the plan would be shared with the Healer Wiseman, who sat on the Tribal Council. Like the Shaman, the Chief Hunter, Trader and Toolmaker were conducting similar meetings to prepare their Wisemen for the meeting.

At the end of the meeting, the Shaman gave us a chance to ask questions. I wanted to learn more about the Tribal Council and how it worked but decided to wait until the meeting ended and ask Mali, for she was the Senior Sorter and understood many things about the tribe that I did not. My first opportunity was when we gathered to discuss the plan. "I think I should be a better teacher," she said, responding to my question. "I am glad you didn't ask that at the meeting. I would have been ashamed of my failure."

"I would not want to embarrass you," I replied.

She continued, "There are five people who sit on the Council: the Tribal Chief and the Wisemen who represent four paths."

"But why do the Healers have a Wiseman and a Shaman too?" I asked.

"Because the Wiseman has climbed the tall mountain, he sees things others may not. Each of the Wisemen have made this climb, and each is a valued counselor to the Tribal Chief. The Shaman has climbed to the top of a smaller mountain and helps us in our daily work to become better at what we do."

I wasn't satisfied yet. "But do the Shaman or the Chief Hunter, or the Chief Trader, or the Chief Toolmaker go to the meeting on the mountain top?"

"No. They are needed here to make important decisions. Should the Council seek advice from one or all of them, they have only to send a runner from the mountain."

"And what of the Elders? Do they ever go?"

"Only when there are significant issues related to their experience. Remember, the most important work is here, not up on the mountain top. The Tribal Chief has said many times that it is the efforts of villagers like you and me who make the tribe prosperous. The Elders can be of greatest value here below because they are wise and have spent much time in the jungle. The Tribal Council and the Chiefs have great respect for their knowledge and experience."

"What do they talk about in the meeting?" Tari asked.

"They make key decisions that affect our survival: supplies, food, clothing, housing. They are concerned with all the needs of the village. They make plans in case something happens: like a fire or a storm. They resolve conflicts among us. This is a very important council."

There were no more questions so we turned our attention to the task of preparing for the meeting with the Shaman. Barto, one of the more experienced Sorters, spoke. "I have noticed lately that the pokeweed berries look withered and dry. I went to the Gatherers just yesterday and asked Lorki if he knew the reason. He said the Hunters knocked them over or cut them down with their machetes when they were tracking the cougars. He said he pointed this out to Bari, one of the Hunters, but he shook his head and walked away."

Nark, a younger Sorter, nodded. "I have wondered about this too. But what is causing it to happen now? We have not had this problem before."

Mali responded. "I think the Hunters are using new trails to track the cougars. I remember something like this happened several years ago. After the Shaman discussed it with the Chief Hunter, things improved for a while. I don't know what they agreed to, but we must ask the Shaman if this new problem should go to the Tribal Council. The pokeweed berries are the best medicine for head parasites, but they cannot be used if they have deteriorated or dried up." We all agreed to ask the Shaman if the Hunters could find a different trail to track the cougars.

Another question arose concerning the Healers in our small village to the north. I perked up because that was where Manu had been sent. It seemed they had located a wonderful source for the rosy periwinkles that cured sore throat, wasp stings and reduced fever but were unwilling to share this information with anyone from our village. Mali felt the Shaman would want to know this, but it probably would be resolved by the Healers and not by the Tribal Council.

That evening at sundown Mali and I met with the Shaman. He listened intently to our concerns. Then he spoke. "I share your concern about the pokeweed berries and will convey this to our Wiseman. Perhaps he can work out something at the Tribal Council. Know this -- if the Council is forced to choose between our needs and those of the Hunters, we cannot expect them to sacrifice food and skins for medicine. Head parasites can be a problem, but they do not threaten one's life. However, we will ask that some concessions be made to help us preserve the pokeweed berries. It is best that we do not demand too much lest we wind up getting nothing."

Then he turned to the other issue concerning the rosy periwinkles. "We can settle that without the Tribal Council. Send Keli to visit Manu. They are friends. Friends can work things out."

Mali was insistent. "They are a small village. They must do as we tell them, mustn't they?"

The Shaman smiled. "Yes, they must. And they will probably tell us where they found the plants. Perhaps next time, they will not search so hard or, if they find the periwinkles in a new place, they will keep silent because they will remember how they were treated. That is why, good intentions often lead to bad results. It's far better to get their willing help. A better question would be 'how did they find the flowers' and not 'where.' Send Keli."

Sandra was so wrapped up in the story that she was surprised when the pilot told the stewardess to prepare for landing. She looked at her watch. It was 3:15. Hopefully she could catch Jack in the office. She had some questions that might impact her meeting in the morning. Stopping at a pay phone, she slid her telephone card into the slot and dialed his number. He was clearly surprised to hear her voice.

"I thought you were on your way to Atlanta."

"I'm there. In an hour I catch my flight to Pembroke. Can you talk for a few minutes?"

"Sure. Everything okay?"

"Yes. I was reading Chapter 6. You had some interesting things to say about 'turf battles.' That's what I want to talk about."

"Shoot."

"The Shaman tells Keli and Mali if the Council is forced to choose between the Hunters and the Healers, the Healers would lose. Does that carry over into PWE?"

"I believe it does. *To understand the 'pecking order' in any organization, look at who gets the most influential positions. If you know their background and where they spent most of their career, you can see who is most likely to prevail.* You see, in a turf battle, the outcome is rarely in doubt. *Human Resources, Finance, and other support organizations can never hope to beat out the Departments that bring in the*

75

money. The exception I can think of is when there are legal or regulatory issues. *Therefore, it really is better not to engage on an unequal battlefield."*

"Are you saying they should always give in?"

"No. If the support organization can come up with a compelling argument that shows their interest takes precedence because it has company-wide implications, it can win. *You've got to realize, though, when you hit the battlefield, you use up your best ammunition. There are times to do that, but beware. 'Silver bullets' are in short supply."*

"So, settle on the front."

"If you can. A lawyer friend of mine once told me a mediocre solution is better than a court battle because you can usually get some concessions if you bargain. If it comes to a fight, then it's winner-take-all. What works for me is to focus on the best outcome. Then, negotiate and expect to concede some things. Now, don't be manipulative and manufacture things to concede. People see right through that strategy. *I've seen more people mess up because they couldn't accept a reasonable compromise that wasn't their idea.* There is a slang expression for that. Perhaps you've heard it: NIH. It means 'not invented here.' I remember once we had two marketing regions trying to put on a common sales campaign. One region wanted to have all the control. When the other came up with a few ideas that wouldn't have changed anything substantially, the first one balked. They refused to accommodate any alterations. In the end, both ran their own campaigns. It was an unreasonable position, and it cost PWE."

Sandra knew of similar situations. "I've seen people fight furiously over small points, even though anyone not emotionally involved could see it was a losing battle and not worth the effort."

Jack agreed. "Someone very wise once told me, *'If it looks like you are going to lose, yield the point willingly and graciously. Collaborate whenever you can. If you can't do that, pick your battles.'* It's foolish to fight over anything unless it is a matter of principle or profit. *And don't forget, it's even more important to be gracious in winning.*

People might forget the outcome, but they never forget how you treated them. Either way, you build up credits, positive or negative."

"You made an interesting point about field offices when you said we can't tell them what to do. On this trip, I feel like Keli being asked to talk to Manu and straighten things out with the village to the north."

"Field offices and headquarters rarely see eye to eye," said Jack. "To the field, headquarters is like an empire wanting to control its subjects from a distance. To headquarters, the field is like a colony, at once asserting independence and at the same time asking for support. The point I was making is *that you cannot control anyone or anything from a distance.* If you don't believe me, try calling your kids when you're on a business trip and telling them to spend the night studying, stay away from the television set and go to bed early. What a joke! If you treat the field like partners rather than take the colonial approach, you can work together. If you don't, they can seem to go along or ignore your requests entirely. Either way you set yourself up for a continuing power struggle."

"I see what you mean. Karen told me about the time she was in charge of a three-person territory in Canada. The boss flew down once every month or two to check on everything. When they gave him bad news, he would fly into a temper. So they quit giving him bad news. In the meantime, he'd call and ask for mountains of information. They finally decided to send him just what they felt would keep him 'off their backs.' Thanks, Jack. I've got a plane to catch and a lot to think about tonight. I might need to consider a little strategy revision before tomorrow. Oh, and by the way, I liked Chapter 6. Are you going to take your readers to the mountain top to hear the Tribal Council in action?"

"That will forever remain a mystery. See you when you get back. I'll be eager to hear how things went."

"And you will. Be back next week. Keep writing. Bye."

Once again in the air, Sandra took out her journal and wrote...

Sandra's Journal

The Sixth Lesson

To survive, choose your battles carefully.
To succeed, understand how conflicts are resolved in your organization.
The secret is, in any conflict people forget who won or lost, but they never forget how you treated them.

"An unlearned carpenter of my acquaintance once said in my hearing:
'There is very little difference between one [person] and another; but what little there is, is very important.'
This distinction seems to go to the root of the matter."
...William James

THE SEVENTH LESSON

On Reputation

It was several weeks before Sandra and Jack got back together, busy weeks with Jack off on an unexpected business trip and Sandra hard at work on several projects. Returning Chapter 6 gave Sandra an opportunity to tell Jack about her trip. She beamed as she recounted how Karen had received several calls from the managers of the field locations commending her and had stopped by her office to thank her for a job well done.

"It's all your doing," Sandra told Jack. "Thank you for all your counseling. I told Karen how supportive you'd been. Guess what! She told me she'd heard of you and what a caring person you are many times. She said I couldn't have chosen a better person to coach me."

"Careful, Sandra. My head is swelling. But don't underrate your achievement -- not to me, to Karen or to the manager. If you received a benefit from some of my experience, don't forget it was you who asked the questions and you who put the answers to good use. I appreciate your giving me a small share of credit *because credit is like a boomerang, the more of it you pass around, the more comes back to you.* You've helped me too, you know. I really enjoy our conversations, not to speak of the discussions on my book. I've got another chapter for you. Will you have time in the next couple of weeks to take a look at it? It's about building a reputation."

"I promise, I'll make time. I can't wait to get your ideas on this. You have a wonderful reputation. It's hard to find anyone who doesn't know you or hasn't heard of you."

…And so, the very next night Sandra kept her promise.

The Four Rings

Seven months had passed since I first met the Elder. I felt I had made a good decision in becoming a Healer and was feeling very comfortable in my Sorting role. Mali was there if I needed her, but I had no difficulty doing my work and often found time to help the others. When Danu, one of the Gatherers, asked me if I would be interested in joining their group, I put him off by telling him that first I wanted to learn everything there was to learn about sorting the leaves and berries.

One afternoon, one of the Sorters, Tari, came to me with a message from the Elder. He had been summoned to a nearby village and would like to see me when he returned the following morning. It was rare for him to send for me. Consequently, I was waiting eagerly when I saw him walking toward me the next morning. We exchanged greetings and I asked when we could get together. He told me he was getting ready for a session with the Wisemen and the Tribal Council. "Tomorrow will be soon enough," he said. Then he pointed toward the hill. "We will go there to see the sun rise."

It was early the next morning when, seated side by side near the top of the hill, we watched as the sun emerged from behind a cloud casting gold and pink ribbons across the morning sky. I did not want to break the silence, but I was eager to hear why the Elder had sent for me. He, on the other hand, seemed content to enjoy the peace of the morning. Finally, he spoke.

"Have you ever wondered what would happen if the sun refused to leave the shelter of the cloud?"

I was perplexed and a bit impatient. "That would never happen. It is natural for the sun to rise in the morning. It cannot stay where it is. It has no choice."

"Nor do you," he responded.

Now I understood. "I just don't feel ready to move. I would have to start all over again. Besides, I'm really good at Sorting and I feel like an important member of the group. Nobody outside the Sorters knows who I am or what I can do."

"Nor do you," he said, once again. Then he added, "*You must make a name for yourself.*"

"How do I do that?"

Picking up a stick, the Elder drew four circles on the ground, each within the other. He pointed to the outermost circle. "The first ring is to demonstrate your skills. *When you become good enough at what you do that others depend upon your judgment, the word will spread and others will hear of you.*"

"But if I stop being a Sorter, then I won't be able to demonstrate my skills."

"You must believe in yourself. You know the roots, fungi, and berries from which we make our medicines. Now it is time to learn to harvest them." Then pointing to the next ring, he said, "*The second way is to demonstrate by your actions that you adhere to a high standard of behavior.*"

"I don't understand. Everyone does, don't they?"

"There are those who wrap themselves in their own needs. They waste much time worrying about the impact of every decision on them. They do not care what goes on in the Tribal Councils unless they hear their names spoken for they feel no responsibility for the welfare of the tribe. If they do the sorting, they think the gathering is unimportant. If they are Hunt-

81

ers, they cannot see the value of Traders. The only questions they ask or answers they listen for are those that affect them directly. They do not handle themselves well in meetings because they cannot listen when others disagree."

"But what does this high standard require?"

"It requires that you strive to do your best in every way and that you think and act for the good of the tribe."

"How can I ever..."

"Keli, think back on all you have done already, and you will believe in yourself as I believe in you. You learn quickly and you are self-disciplined. You do not waste the hours. You listen when others speak. You withhold angry words even when you do not agree. There are other things you will learn, but you will learn them easily because you are a good student. *Go to the tribal meetings. Watch how the Shaman and the Wiseman act and do likewise.* When people see you do these things, they will take note and your name will be honored."

I understood. "Then what is the third ring?"

"It is the way you treat others," he said. "People remember how you treat them, and they carry this with them forever. *When others speak of you, let it be for the way you care, whether it's the Tribal Chief or the smallest child.*"

Then he pointed to the innermost circle. "This one is *purpose.* *If you would make a place for yourself, you must know what your mission is.*"

"But what if I don't know my purpose?" I asked. "How do I find it?"

"Look at the sun. Every day it makes its journey across the sky. You are on a journey too. Listen to your thoughts, examine your heart and be guided by what they tell you. If you shot an arrow, you would know when it found the mark. In the same way, when the time is right, you'll come to understand how you can best serve the Korios and yourself. People will then seek your counsel and be silent when you speak."

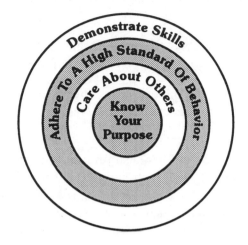

"Which of the rings is the most important?" I asked.

"They are all important," said the Elder. *"If you cannot demonstrate the skill, why would anyone seek your advice? If you are not seen as placing the tribe first, who would value your counsel? If you are not caring, who will care about you? And if you do not know what you are looking for, how will you know when you find it? All are required if you wish others to call your name."*

I pondered his words for a time. I knew he was right and that I would have to leave the safety and comfort of my group of friends to test myself and make my place. For a long time neither of us spoke. This time I broke the silence and asked the Elder to tell me about his long service as a Healer. In this manner, we passed the rest of the day. The Elder had held many different jobs and enjoyed every aspect of the work. When he told about some of his adventures as a Gatherer, I was intrigued. We ate of the tender orange fruit of the hogplum tree as I listened to stories of the cures that had enabled many of my fellow tribesmen to lead long and productive lives. By the end of the day, I had made up my mind to make the change. As the sun set, both of us were aware of the significance it had for the two observing it --- one at the beginning of the journey, one much closer to the end. Then we rose and walked together down the hillside and toward the village.

"I'd like to talk about the circles," said the note in the middle of Jack's desk. "Give me a call if you have time for lunch today."

He did have time, and two hours later, seated by the window in the company cafeteria, Sandra and Jack were in the midst of a discussion of Chapter 7.

"When I talk about 'demonstrating skill' in the story, I'm basically talking about showing you have excellent technical skills. My point is this: *Having technical skills means very little if no one is aware of them.* You need to make them known. *The trick is to do that without seeming to blow your own horn.* Provide a report to the boss, offer to serve on a project team, give a short presentation at a meeting. Do something, but whatever you do, don't close your office door and do it in the dark."

"You mean the way I used to do it when I expected to be rewarded for hard work."

"Exactly. I found the second concept a bit more difficult to explain in the story, only because certain words and ideas don't fit with my jungle theme. Not that I haven't taken some liberties here and there," added Jack with a chuckle. "The idea I'm talking about is professionalism, which is a very broad term. It includes everything from the way you present your ideas to another group to how effectively you take charge of your time. It's handling yourself well in conflict situations or running a group meeting. It's considering things from the perspective of what's good for the team, or the company rather than being self-absorbed. It's knowing how to say no -- and do it gracefully."

"I like the way you explained that as adhering to a high standard of behavior."

"Well, I hope it wasn't too much of a stretch. I might add some thoughts there if you think it necessary."

"I don't think so. I really did understand it, but how do you distinguish that from the third ring -- how you treat others? Don't most business books put them together as interpersonal skills?"

"Some do. I see them as different. Let's say you have top-notch technical skills and are very good at resolving conflicts and presenting your ideas. My feeling is you're fifty to sixty percent of the way home. But how other people respond to you makes a big difference. Whether you call it interpersonal skills or likeability, it impacts how quickly people return your calls and how eager they are to put you on their committees or project teams. If you're the leader, it shows in the enthusiasm with which people follow you. It also determines the kind of information they share with you. Look, Sandra, if you had to choose between two equally qualified people to work with you, and one had a reputation for caring about people and the other didn't, who would you choose?"

"No contest. I'd go with the one who cared. Then I'd know if I had a problem, I'd have someone who would listen. Now let's go to the real reason I wanted to talk. That's the inside circle, the one you call *purpose*. I think I understand what you were talking about. It's knowing what you are trying to achieve, isn't it?"

"Yes. Without *purpose* everything you do is an activity. Some activities are successful, some aren't. Now you can have many different goals and feel very good about achieving them -- but in support of what? That's what you have to consider."

"I mean, you're not talking about a higher purpose, are you, Jack?"

"Not in the religious or spiritual sense. I think that's important, but it's outside the province of this book, although I do think your work life is an extension of other parts of your life. There are people who check their personal selves at the door when they walk into the building. This can create a conflict -- one they may not be aware of. But in this book, I'm focusing my attention on what work is about. You see, you are more likely to hit the target when you know what you're aiming at. And, if you want to make a name for yourself, it answers the question -- what name?"

The Seventh Lesson

To survive, make your contributions visible.
To succeed, combine high standards of professional behavior
  toward business with caring behavior toward people
The secret is, if you want to build your reputation, choose how you
  want to be remembered.

> "Culture is not life in its entirety,
> but just the moment of security,
> strength, and clarity."
> ...José Ortega y Gasset

THE EIGHTH LESSON

On Getting Things Through the System

Jack hung up the phone and watched his computer going through its morning ritual, the start-up screen winking and blinking with obscure messages. For a moment he closed his eyes and daydreamed about the last two weeks in Maui. His days had been divided between collecting seashells on the beach with Laura and long sunny afternoons, when after their morning swim, he had leaned back in the lounge chair and thought about the book. Laura, who loved to visit the shopping areas, had been most accommodating, giving Jack several hours of free time to write in the afternoons. Now he was eager to meet with Sandra and talk about the book.

Sandra was anything but relaxed. She was working on a special project that could impact the pricing system for several PWE products and had spent the last two weeks in conferences and meetings followed by three days working feverishly in her office. Jack's phone call this morning had come as a welcome break. Grabbing her coffee cup, she headed toward the elevator and from there made her way to his office.

One hand on her hip, and shaking her head in mock disgust, Sandra stood in the doorway to Jack's office. "You look entirely too rested to me. Here I was up to my eyebrows in pressure, running here, running there, tossing and turning every night while you and Laura were lying on gigantic beach towels, sopping up the sand and the sea.

I'll bet the worst pressure of the trip was deciding where to have dinner every night."

"Enough!" said Jack, laughing as he handed her a small package containing the necklace Laura had purchased for her on one of her afternoon expeditions. "Let me buy my way out of this."

Sandra smiled as she held up the double strand of pink seashells. "Thanks, Jack," she said. "Please thank Laura and tell her I love it."

"Okay, okay," said Jack. "Your turn. Tell me what you've been up to."

He listened intently as Sandra told of the proposed new system of pricing. She had just completed the study she told him. As she concluded, she held up two crossed fingers "So far, so good. But wish me luck!"

"This is great!" he told her. "This will give you a lot of visibility. You've earned it. And you don't need any luck."

"I wish I were as confident as you," responded Sandra with a sigh. "If work and effort would do it, we'd be home free. Right now the odds of approval are fifty-fifty at best."

"Who has to approve it?"

"Only the top level of our Marketing managers: that's Allen Rankin, Mary Standish, Carl Francis, and Phyllis Cohen. They can be tough, Jack."

"Of course they can be, and they should be," he said. "Otherwise, good projects like yours would take a back seat as everyone pushed their own agendas. Will they support you?"

Sandra shrugged her shoulders. "I wish I knew."

"You need to get some idea before the meeting. We'll get back to that in a minute. If they like it, can they approve it?"

"I'm not sure, Jack. It may need to go to the Management Council."

"You need to know that before the meeting too. *Making a formal proposal without knowing what kind of support you have and what obstacles are out there is like going into battle without a shield or a sword. It's possible to survive anyway, but you wind up with more scars.*"

Sandra nodded, "I see what you mean," she said. "But how do I get that information."

"Have I got a deal for you!"

"I'll bet it's Chapter 8." she laughed. "Hand it over and let's talk tomorrow. You've planted some seeds and I want to talk about how to grow them."

This time Sandra didn't wait to go home. If Chapter 8 could help, she wanted to start on it immediately.

The Plan

Our group of Gatherers was dejected as we walked toward the village. We had spent three days searching for the golobe fungus without any luck. Before we left, Tolar had reminded us how important it was to harvest it before the rainy season. The medicines to cure infections were vital to the health of every villager, and our supplies were running dangerously low. Tolar ran to meet us as we approached the village. When he saw our empty baskets, the disappointment we felt was reflected on his face. The Elder Healers must meet tomorrow at sunrise, he told us, to decide what to do. I had been thinking about this day and night as we searched the forests for the plants and wondered if we might trade one of the other tribes some skins, meat or medicine for the supplies to keep us going until we found the fungus.

Tolar thought about it for a moment. Then he nodded. "It would be good to go to the Elders with a plan," he said. "Talk to other villagers today, Keli. The Traders and the Hunters often run into tribes from the valley or across the river. See if you can learn from them which tribes might be willing to help us and what we could trade them. Then we could go to the meeting tomorrow and you could ask the Elder Healers about this."

I was excited and a little nervous about the prospect of being heard at such an important meeting. But who should I talk to? And what should I say? I went to see The Elder. He was talking to several of the Traders, but he motioned for me to join them. I stood back until they had finished talking. When they moved away, I told him what had happened.

We strolled toward the river, and for a moment, he seemed lost in thought. Then he turned to me and said, "You have posed a good solution, Keli, and one the Elders would be interested in hearing more about. It pleases me because you have the Korios' interests at heart and because Tolar has shown great confidence in you. What would you learn from me?"

"I'm not sure what I should do next. I know I could ask Tolar, but I'm afraid he will think I am not wise, if I do."

"Ah, but you are wise. Those who are not act without thinking. *It is far wiser to admit you do not know and seek help than to act as if you know and thus fail to receive it.*" He paused for a moment, then added, "If you want the Elders to listen when you speak, you must understand the ways of the tribe."

"What ways do you mean?" I asked.

"First, you must be sure of what you speak. Seek knowledge from those who have walked the same path so when you speak to the Elders, they will see that you are wise."

"How do I do that? Tolar told me to ask the Hunters and the Traders, but there's so little time. Who should I talk to? I know Pardo and Kodi. Both are Traders. Should I go to them?"

"*No, for neither of them sits near the seat of power.* You have met Talu, the Elder. Because he sits close to the Chief Trader, he is a better choice. What will you offer him?"

"My attention and respect."

"Good. Now, which of the Hunters do you know?"

"I could ask Bari. We have walked the path many times before we separated, he to go to the Hunt and I to gather medicine plants. He knows the Hunter Wiseman well, and he could help me."

"Then he is a good choice. Also, when you wait to speak tomorrow, show the Elder Healers great respect. Sit patiently without speaking while we lay out our concerns. Then, allow Tolar to speak before you. He will tell us you wish to speak, but you should remain silent. You must wait for all the Elders to acknowledge you first. *Notice what words the Elders use and do not use when addressing one another.* You will see that no one uses the word 'I' for we Elders disdain it. As you describe the plan, you must ask for our counsel. These are the ways that show the proper respect for experience, age and wisdom and they are required of you."

"Now tell me more about your plan," he continued. "Who would we send to meet with these other tribes to work on a trade, or would you ask the Elders to decide who should go?"

"There are others with greater wisdom who must make this decision. Will you support me in the meeting?"

"I will, Keli. *It is also most important to know before the meeting if the other two Elder Healers will support you or if not, for what reasons they might oppose the trade, for then you can decide what you need to say to them. If they support you, you will want to spend most of the time describing the plan; if they do not, you must spend most of it showing how the tribe will benefit.* By doing this, you will grow in the Elder Healers' eyes for you are showing respect for their time and the weight of the decisions they bear."

"But I thought the meeting was to get their support."

"Ah, my young friend, such *meetings are rarely arranged to get support. Rather, they are a necessary means of demonstrating that support you already have.*"

"Then how will I find out if they will support or oppose the trade?"

"There are several ways. The best way is to visit them after you have talked with Bari and Talu. If you do not feel you know them well enough or for some other reason cannot see them, you must find other sources who know them well, perhaps a friend who sits beside them as you do me; perhaps Tolar. Use this information to prepare yourself for the meeting."

"You sit beside them in the meetings. What can you tell me?"

"Only this much: Cossi will wonder which Traders and Hunters you spoke with and what concerns they had; Balar will be most interested in the details of your plan."

I paused for a moment, thinking. Then I looked intently at the Elder. "Father, tell me honestly, am I making a mistake? Will they think me a fool?"

"I cannot say what others will think. But this I know, my son, I will be proud of you for showing that you are willing to take a stand, even at the risk of looking foolish."

I had no more questions. We walked back in silence, the Elder enjoying the beauty of the day and I, lost in thought about the many things I must do before the meeting. The closer we got to the village, the more my confidence grew. Thanks to the Elder, I had a plan -- and when I spoke to the Elder Healers the next day, he would be there to support me. As we parted, I was struck by how generous and caring he was and how much I had learned from him. I turned to tell him, but he was watching a mother bird feeding her nestling, and I was hesitant to disturb the serenity I observed on his face.

Sandra reread the last page of Chapter 8 as she waited for Jack in his office. He had called saying he would be a few minutes late this morning due to some unexpected misbehavior on the part of his cherished 1939 Packard. Walking briskly into his office, he was momentarily startled to find Sandra seated at the small conference table near the door. "OOPS, sorry," he said. "The old boy was acting up again."

"No problem," she grinned. "Just start his engine with coffee. This is the second cup you've bought me this morning and I'm raring to go. I want to talk about *Secrets* and my little project."

Now it was Jack's turn to smile. "I'll make you a deal. I'll do it for a cup of coffee."

"Check your cup warmer, my friend. It's done. Reading the story made me realize why it's important to be prepared, and I've already tapped into some sources to find out how much support I have on the Marketing Council. So far so good. Now, here's what I'm wondering. You talked about 'observing the rules.' What message is there in that for me and the situation I'm in?"

"Sandra, if you want to be successful in this or any other organization, *you must learn the unspoken rules. That involves understanding the way things are done.* These unspoken rules or protocols lie deeply entrenched in every facet of the way organizations conduct their internal business. They underlie the way the organization communicates, how it dispenses information, how it makes key decisions. Those who violate these protocols are seldom successful."

"*Every organization has its protocols of communication.* This regards everything from who speaks to whom to the choice of words used in meetings or in any formal business situation. For example, before I came here, Reed and Connors, the company I worked for, had subjects and even words that were taboo. We never used them because management was highly sensitive to them and let us know it. Once I was in a meeting and heard someone describe a pilot project as a *failure*. You wouldn't have believed the scowls and looks of disapproval. Finally, the manager told her never to use that word again. This was not a failure, he told her. It was only a *limited success*."

Sandra laughed. "A limited success!"

"I'm serious," said Jack. "Another protocol at R&C regarded questioning management decisions, particularly in a meeting. It just was not allowed. I soon understood that R&C managers were regarded as much smarter than we were. While often this was true, it prevented us from continuing to search for the best solutions."

Sandra shook her head. "It sure is different at PWE."

"Every organization is different, Sandra, *but if you really want to be successful there you recognize the protocol. Once you step beyond it, you may achieve results -- but they are likely to be the wrong ones.* Besides topics and words, another implicit rule or protocol of communication involves the direction it flows in the company. In more open organizations, it moves up, down and sideways. In more closed organizations it tends to flow one way, down. At PWE, when management sends out an employee questionnaire, it openly discusses the results and involves employees in plans to work on problem areas. At R&C, surveys were sent out yearly, but management never revealed the results or involved employees in any plans. I truly believe management considered what was said, but they saw no reason to communicate their decisions to us because the protocol at R&C fostered one-way communication."

Jack continued, "Now based on what you learn about the protocol, you can begin to understand what management's attitude toward communication is, and this is very important. *If management uses honest and direct communication with employees, and encourages straight responses, then we can say management's attitude is very open. That means, if you are in a meeting, it's okay to take issue with someone's ideas, even if that someone is higher up in the organization.* That's PWE's communication attitude. At R&C, management's attitude was that communication was used to achieve a specific result. Employees there spent a great deal of time working and reworking every word in their presentations to management. Management, in turn, spent a great deal of its time working and reworking its communication with employees."

"Doesn't that speak volumes about mutual trust?"

"It probably does, but Sandra, the important thing is when you meet with the Marketing Managers you will need to observe PWE protocol by being very straightforward about the pluses and minuses of your proposal."

"I have three questions," said Sandra. "Number one, you mentioned information and decision making as well as communication. Are these the only areas where protocols exist?"

"No way," said Jack. "There are dress protocols, many including not only styles but acceptable fabrics, cuts, and designers. There are office appearance protocols like sizes and types of desks, choices of plants and pictures. Those are just examples. There are many others. But information and decision making rules can be particularly subtle. Take information, for example. In some organizations, everyone knows what is going on, and people have easy access to information about almost anything. Some companies even open their management meetings to employees. Other organizations hold information more tightly. People are excluded from management meetings and rarely find out what happened in them unless management identifies this to be a need. But what I'm describing are the extremes. Most organizations, like ours, fall somewhere in between. The protocol also involves when people receive information -- that is, how close to the time it is learned by management that it becomes available to everyone, if it ever does."

"So from that, you can figure out what management's attitude toward information is. *In open organizations, management trusts employees to hear both good and bad news because it believes that knowledge enables everyone to be more productive. This is usually typical of flatter organizations. In closed organizations, management withholds sensitive information because it fears that it will fall into the wrong hands or that people won't be able to handle the truth for one reason or another.* This is most typical in multi-layered organizations where people equate knowledge with power."

"Decision making protocols are exactly the same," continued Jack. "In open organizations, decisions are made at the lowest levels in the organization. The attitude is that the people most closely involved in the work have the most information. In closed organizations, the decisions are the sole prerogative of management. In those companies, there is a feeling that since information is not widely handed out, the workers are not in a position to know. Again, those are extremes. Most companies fall somewhere in between. The more bureaucratic a company is, the more it tends to push decision making up. What was your second question, Sandra?"

"If a company is closed in one area, as in releasing information, does it necessarily follow that it will be closed in all three?"

"Well, it's a matter of degree. A company may be completely closed in the way it provides information but a bit more open in communication to employees. At the same time, you can see why they would work hand in hand. A free flow of information generally encourages good communication. The more information people have and the more they share it, the more likely they will offer good suggestions. When that happens, organizations begin to see how helpful it is to get input from everyone before making a key decision. And that works the other way too. When people don't know the important things that are happening around them and there is no formal means of upward communication, they lack the information or channels to input their ideas or suggestions. Therefore, management decides. One thing about closed companies -- sometimes they are much more organized, and far less sloppy than open companies."

"Yes," said Sandra, "but are they as creative?"

"No, they're not. Sometimes being creative is not considered a high value. The important thing is, *you need to understand the protocol or you can find yourself operating like a refuge from a closed system in an open one, or vice versa.*"

"Okay, Jack. Now for the grand prize, my third question. If you work in a more closed company, how do you communicate and get information? Also, how can you influence decisions?"

"I think that's two questions. On the first question, in closed companies, people observe the protocols in formal situations, but there are informal customs that apply as well. For example, at R&C when people were in formal meetings, they never spoke of *problems*. In fact, laughingly, we called *problems*, the *p-word*. The real meetings usually happened after the formal meetings were over. Then people congregated in their offices, closed the door and interpreted what the events in the meeting meant. Sometimes, friendly managers would come in and share some insights informally with us. There is much more use of the informal systems in closed environments like R&C than there are in open ones like PWE. *So if you understand the protocol and the attitude in a closed environment, you use the informal system to get at underlying messages.* See what I mean?"

"I do. What about information?" Sandra asked.

"No matter how an organization is, people need and want information. In open organizations, the protocol works. People are encouraged to share information freely. If you don't know something, anything, it's easy to find it out. *In a closed organization, you need a good network, one which includes people in management who know what's going on.* If you don't have one, you're subject to hanging out with those who spend great amounts of their time spreading idle gossip and rumors. This leads to speculations with few bases in fact. And gossip and rumors are like whirlpools. They suck you in, but there's neither light nor air down there. That's why *people who live and work in closed organizations should avoid taking part in these things or give much credence to them.*"

"I agree," said Sandra. "I've heard lots of speculations and wild rumors that have never come true. Sometimes I think they are based on wishful thinking."

Jack nodded. "Actually, the people who spread the rumors or engage in speculation rarely know what's really going on. *In fact, the rule of thumb is, those who know the most, usually say the least.* Instead, use your powers of observation and your understanding of the organization's protocol and attitudes to learn what you need to know. Then turn to good networks to confirm the facts. *Above all, never participate in gossip, rumors, or idle speculation. The mud they generate often adheres to you.*"

"I suppose there are protocols that apply to decisions as well," said Sandra. Jack nodded. "I have a friend that works in a closed environment," she continued. "I wonder if she can influence decisions when they are made at the top."

Jack smiled, "So now you are mentoring your friend, eh? I like that. Decision making protocol is related to organization charts and hierarchies. Within these frameworks are the practices of each organization. How much authority and control is exercised by the top? What level of decision can the employee make? Even in closed companies your friend can have influence. The secret goes back to what we talked about in creating a good reputation. *Once you earn the respect of those who go to the meetings where decisions are made, they tend to value your input.* That again is more a custom than a protocol. There are people in every organization who are thought leaders. That is, they may not have the decision-making power, but they are widely respected and consulted by those who do. When those people know who you are, what you know, and what you stand for, they in turn will seek you out."

"Like they seek you out," interrupted Sandra. "I've seen that many times."

"Just like that. In formal systems, you're anointed. You kind of earn your place and the right to be involved in the informal system. There's just one more point. Sandra, *you have to be willing to put your stake in the ground.* You've got to show there are things you believe in strongly enough to stand up and be counted."

"Isn't that risky? I mean if you take a strong stand, mightn't that affect your ability to influence decisions?"

"That's true. So you need to be thoughtful in the exercise of that. But if you want to have influence, people need to have a sense that you stand somewhere -- and if you are never willing to take a risk in the name of something worthwhile, then why should they seek your input. I have a friend in another PWE region who had very strong beliefs in the use and distribution of computers. Long before PWE adopted these attitudes and provided these computers, it wasn't fashionable, or wise, to take that position. Over the long haul, he's been proven right, and management sees him as forward looking."

"I'm glad that you can influence closed organizations," said Sandra, "but I think PWE is a bit more open in its decision making, don't you think?"

"A bit," said Jack knowing where this was leading.

"And yet," continued Sandra, "I've learned when it comes to the pricing project I'm involved in, the decision will most likely be made by the Marketing Managers followed by the endorsement of the Management Council. I guess that's a protocol, right?"

"You got it," said Jack.

"So tell me, Jack, is Keli going to be successful in the meeting?"

"Of course he is. Didn't he get good advice and act on it? And besides, in *Secrets* it's the author's prerogative to make everything come out right."

"Wish you were writing my story. Then I could be one hundred per cent sure this project would be approved."

"What do you think so far?" asked Jack. "I know you've been checking on how much support you have from the Marketing Managers."

"Things look good. But then, I'm like Keli. I get good advice and I follow it."

Sandra's Journal

The Eighth Lesson

To survive, learn the organization's communication, information, and decision-making protocols.
To succeed, tap into the informal system.
The secret is, if you want influence, you have to put your stake in the ground.

"Intelligence is quickness to apprehend as distinct from ability, which is capacity to act wisely on the thing apprehended."
...Alfred North Whitehead

THE NINTH LESSON

On Major Changes and Upheavals

It was like being in the midst of a thunderstorm. Rumors of reorganization swept through PWE like lightning bolts. Talk of layoffs echoed like distant thunder. People were anxious. They saw managers scurrying to meetings behind closed doors. After the meetings, they heard nothing. It was rumored they were there to determine the fate of departments, field units and even individual employees. Telltale signs of concern were the frequent small gatherings in many offices. Doors were shut and conversations were in whispers.

Behind one of these doors on the eighth floor Sandra paced as she told Jack what she had heard. Then with a sigh, she dropped down into a handy chair -- and waited.

Several moments passed before Jack spoke. "Okay," he said, "so you've heard there's going to be a reorganization at PWE. You're not sure if it's to be the whole company or specific departments -- but you hear the company will reduce layers of management and downsize and whole areas will be outsourced. Does that sum it up?"

"Pretty much," she replied. "Jack, I don't like this and I don't know what to do."

"And you came to me because..."

"Because I don't know how much of it is true, and you always know what's going on."

"How much of what you've told me is rumor and what part, if any, is fact?"

"I've gotten it from my network, more or less. Admittedly, it's mostly rumor -- but my sources (who shall remain anonymous, per instructions from you) are in different departments and the rumors are too similar to be discounted."

"Sandra, that doesn't prove anything. There's one thing you can be sure of -- if a rumor is exciting, the informal network, or grapevine, can move it as fast as the speed of sound. To be fair, I've gotten a sense that change is in the works, too. In fact, I've been writing about it in Chapter 9, which I'm going to give you to read. Give me a few days and I'll find out what I can. I'll call you when I have some info. In the meantime, my best advice is to *be cool and that means try to stay away from the small clusters of people hanging out in offices trading rumors*. No matter what changes are made eventually, there is still work to be done. Don't seek out more answers yet, and above all, *don't contribute to the misinformation that's floating around.*"

Sandra felt better. She reached for Chapter 9, promising to await Jack's call. As she walked out, she paused in the doorway to his office. "When we talk, will you tell me how you figured out change is in the works? I'm wondering if you heard rumors too or if there are other ways."

"I will," said Jack. "And you're right. There are other ways -- more reliable than rumors. Think of them as drumbeats. I'll call."

That night, Sandra took out Chapter 9.

The Storm

A storm was brewing. Even before the thunder intensified, even before the clouds darkened, I could sense it was different from the typical jungle storms -- and far more menacing.

First were the days when the faint echoes of thunder vibrated like drum beats from afar. They were followed by nights with no breeze at all when a pervasive stillness hung in the air. The birds, insects and animals of the jungle seemed to know of the approaching storm long before the thunder and lightning threatened the village. All the normal jungle sounds, the hoarse "brr" of the tanagers, the staccato shriek of parakeets, the shrill hum of the beetles, the screeching of the spider monkeys increased in volume and intensity. The rustling in the trees and on the ground signaled a restlessness and movement that I could feel in every pore of my body.

When the storm hit, I was awed by its ferocity. First came the lightning -- in flashes of energy that seemed to pierce the skies and create an eerie glow over the village. It was followed by the thunder rising from a faint rumble to a deafening roar that seemed to shake the earth beneath my feet. I wanted to move, to run -- but I was transfixed by the sheer power of the storm. A crackling sound followed by loud cries jolted me from this trance-like state. It was fire -- the village was in flames. Silhouettes appeared in the darkness as villagers hurriedly gathered possessions and raced toward the river. "Keli, Keli --- hurry!" It was Mali. She grabbed my hand -- but I hung back.

"The Elder -- where's the Elder?"

"Over there," she said, pointing toward the clearing. "He sent me to get you."

He was directing excited villagers toward the hill and away from the river, sending others with messages to the chiefs and Wisemen when Mali and I reached his side. "Carry these," he said, gesturing toward baskets of foliage, "and run to the hill."

"But what about you?" I protested. He was already engaged in animated conversation with Pola and I could see he would give me no more attention. So we ran, Mali and I, with baskets of healing plants and berries in our arms, toward the hill. That night we returned many times, too many to count, to

103

salvage other precious supplies. Then came the dawn when exhausted, we lay down at the edge of the hill.

Our sleep was short and disturbed by the drops of rain-- at first gentle, then increasingly persistent. Tired and soaked, we sought shelter beneath the canopy of trees surrounding the remains of the village and surveyed the scene. The fire was out, but most of the village had been reduced to smoldering heaps of ashes. Around the remains stood disconsolate groups of villagers -- some talking, some weeping, others sifting through the ashes in search of some special treasure left behind.

We saw a group of Healers and hurried to join them. "What's going on?" I asked. "What are we going to do?"

"We're going to rebuild the village, right here," said a young Sorter.

"No, no," said one of the Gatherers. "The Tribal Council and the Elders are meeting right now to decide where to go."

"Some of us will be moved to other villages," said a third Healer. "We don't know whether we will go or stay. Maybe some of us will have to go to another place."

"Or stay with another tribe," said a fourth.

I felt myself becoming anxious as we stood there talking to the Healers in the ruins of the village. Mali must have sensed how I was feeling. "Let's go, Keli," she said. "We will look for Pola. She usually knows before anyone what the Tribal Council is planning."

As we walked toward the pond, Mali stopped suddenly. "There! Look there!" she said pointing to the clearing on the other side of the water. I saw the village Elders, the Wisemen, and the Chiefs huddled together. Pola was sitting beside the pond not far from the Tribal Council. She motioned for us to join her. Her smile was a warm and welcome contrast to the dismal and depressive atmosphere we had just left.

"There are all kinds of stories being told out there, Pola," I said, "but which of them are true? One person said we will rebuild the village right here. Someone else said the whole tribe might have to move away. Then I heard we might even be asked to stay with another tribe. I don't know what to think. I'm worried." Mali nodded her agreement.

Pola listened intently. Finally she took my hand and Mali's and said, "Keli, Mali -- I don't want you to worry about this. The Tribal Council and Elders are wise. They have been through many misfortunes and they know what to do. They have been meeting through the night and all of the morning debating and discussing many different options. Soon they will call us together to tell us what has been decided. One thing the Elder told me early this morning -- it is likely that some of us will stay here and rebuild the village. The rest will probably go to our small northern village."

"Where Manu is?" I asked.

"Yes," replied Pola. "They are meeting now to decide who will stay here and who will go."

I felt better now because I trusted Pola and now had more information. I thought about the other Healers and how knowing this might help them too. "Do you want me to go back and tell the others?" I asked.

Pola thought for a moment. Then she responded, "That's a good idea, Keli, but let's wait a little while. I want to find out if there will be any big changes in this plan first. We won't wait long though. If the Tribal Council is not finished by the time the sunbeams strike the hill, we will tell the others what we know."

"How will the Council decide who goes and who stays?" asked Mali. "Will we have a choice?"

"I'm not sure," said Pola. "What is most likely -- and don't depend on this -- is that some of our leaders will go and some will stay. Some of the tribe will be asked to stay or go based on need and others will be able to volunteer. But that's just my guess."

"I hope the three of us stay together," said Mali. "I don't mind going or staying, but I don't want to lose my friends."

105

"What would happen if we three volunteered to go? Could we do that?" I wondered.

Pola nodded. "Maybe we could. But I think we should consider the good of the village first. Let's see where they need the most help. Then the three of us can volunteer for that, whatever *that* is."

"What if the Tribal Council has already decided?" asked Mali. "Do you think we can get them to change their minds?"

"They are great leaders. They are also very wise," said Pola. "If there is a way they can accommodate our needs, they will surely do that. Perhaps we should approach the Elder. He will help us if he can."

Mali stayed with Pola and I returned to the hillside to sort through the baskets. There would be time enough for plans later. Now we needed to know what remained of our store of healing materials. It appeared that we had salvaged a good supply of pokeweed berries, ipoh roots and konoyah leaves, enough to last for several weeks.

When I went back to the pond to give Pola and Mali the good news, I was greeted by two sad faces. The Elder was leaving. He would be gone for many months journeying though the jungle gathering supplies from other tribes to replace those we had lost in the fire. I was stunned. "No, it can't be so!" I depended on him for so much, and I loved him like a father. "Perhaps he will take me with him," I said. "I'll talk to him. It will be all right."

I felt Pola's arm around my shoulder. "It isn't to be, Keli. The Wisemen have decided. There is much to be done here. You are young and strong. We need you to help rebuild the village. Your knowledge and skills have been recognized. You are to become the Head Gatherer."

"But I could talk to them," I said. "He cannot go alone. He needs someone young like me to help him."

"He will be traveling with three Hunters and two Traders. It is decided."

I was bereft.

"I know how Keli feels," said Sandra as she stepped inside Jack's office and closed the door. "We'll be losing some people if there is a downsizing, and -- well, it's going to hurt."

"Of course, it will."

"Okay, Jack. You said you've got some news. Shoot!"

"There will be a downsizing. My sources say it should be announced in just two weeks. I understand PWE management will be reduced to three layers."

"What about the rest of us? How many...?"

"The best number I could get was six to seven percent."

Sandra groaned. "That's about one hundred people."

"I know."

"So what are the chances it could happen to me?"

"Sandra, nobody can ever know for sure. I think they are very small. You are well respected in both HR and Marketing. See, the Healers and Traders both like you," he added with a grin.

"That's not funny," she said, trying to hide a slight smile. "All right, Jack...so I'd make it in the jungle."

"You're in the jungle now."

"So how do people survive times like these -- with everything spinning around?" asked Sandra. "I don't like change. It always comes along just when you're getting comfortable."

"Well, when Keli meets with the Elder, he will learn the six key steps to doing well even in a rapidly changing environment. And, I'll save you the trouble of asking what they are....

Step One is gather information. As soon as people suspect change is in the wind, they begin to speculate. *The most important thing you*

107

can do at this time is to pick up data from people who would be likely to know the most."

"Another reason to have a good network."

"Right. There will always be rumors, gossip, and some interesting signals, if you can read them."

"Are those the drumbeats you mentioned earlier."

"They are. For example: there are a lot of clues from the external environment that change is afoot. That's one extra reason to read business journals as well as the business pages of a reliable newspaper. If reorganizations, buyouts or outsourcings are happening in other companies within the industry, it is a pretty good indication that we'll experience similar changes before long. After all, the same market issues and economic circumstances apply to all of us. So, look for industry trends, economic indicators and the like."

"The internal clues are there as well -- but they're often harder to read. Some things I have noticed in PWE: before there is any major change announced, there are usually management speeches about how we have to do something about staffing or productivity -- and we need to be thinking about how we're going to get to the next milestone. Things like that. Then there is usually a flurry of meetings at higher levels. Often these are offsite. In fact, you'll see some rather strange combinations of managers going -- that is, people who rarely attend the same meetings. Sometimes a new training program, one that deals with work processes (like re-engineering), is announced. People are selected to be trained, or everyone is lined up for the classes. Occasionally there are consultants, more than usual, brought in. Some of these are people who specialize in work productivity, reorganizations or outsourcing. *During this period, if you ask for information you are likely to get less than usual. Don't spend too much time worrying about it. Just begin to look for some answers."*

"All I feel in this situation is helpless."

"But you needn't be, Sandra. Once you begin to form some ideas about what might be happening, talk with a couple of key people in your network. Tell them what you suspect. Ask them if they have heard anything they can talk about, in confidence. If they haven't heard, they'll usually tell you that. But don't think that means it won't happen. If they have heard but can't talk, you can usually make some assumptions by their failure to deny it. *If you've developed relationships built on confidence and trust, you'll get information in some form.* Just stay tuned in. *The most important thing to remember is to focus on what you can control.* Throughout the process, pay attention -- and continue to look for data points."

"So let's move on to Step Two. That's an important mental process called Anticipating. It's messy, but it's crucial. You sit down and ask yourself: 'What would happen if...? What's the worst thing that could happen? What's the likelihood of it happening? How would it affect the business? How would it affect me?'"

"But Jack, if you don't know for sure, how would that help?"

"Look, people are always anxious in a time of change. But sometimes if you think about things, you realize there is little reason for your anxiety. Then you can put your worries aside. But, let's take the worst case. Suppose there is reason to be anxious. Sitting around and waiting -- or worse, building your anxiety by compounding it with others' anxieties, won't help at all. *The universal balm is action.* So think of anticipation as the way to get started. And that brings us to Step Three: action planning."

"To begin with, consider things you can do to influence the outcome. This might include talking to your supervisor about a move or a temporary assignment into another part of the company. It could also involve calling a couple of key people in your network and letting them know you are looking for an opportunity. Find out what is going on in their areas. Someone who has mentored you might be a good resource at this time. No matter what the outcome is, don't panic. What you are doing is quietly assessing your options."

"Next: *prepare yourself for the possibility of a job search by updating your resume and contacting your external network. This is a good time to gather financial data -- to consider how you would man-*

age this important aspect of your life in case of a job search. Alert family members to the potential situation and enlist their support."

"Third, it won't hurt to circulate your resume through your external network -- and beyond. You might also do a little research as you consider what placement agencies might be viable choices for you. At this point you need to do some serious thinking about your priorities and your career. What do you really want? Have your priorities changed? Maybe you planned to stay with one company, but now you see an opportunity to do something else. Do you want to go back to school? Stay home? Or open your own business? What is important to you in making a career decision? What are the important qualifications for a new position? *Be sure to differentiate between needs and wants.* Would you be interested -- or willing -- to relocate? To consider related fields? What are your capabilities? What areas of work would interest you? These are the critical questions you must answer as you develop your plan."

"Now, with an action plan in hand, continue to do the high-quality work you're getting paid for. In periods of change, people sometimes focus so much attention on their fears that little gets done. Be supportive to your friends, but remember you are still on the payroll. That's not just being loyal to the company. It's being loyal to the professional you are. *Be sure to keep your own counsel about your plans.* By taking these steps, you should have increased your sense of control and reduced your anxiety level."

"Step Four is to *stay alert to possibilities and opportunities.* Continue to gather data by keeping your eyes and ears open. Keep in touch with those network members who have shown a willingness to help you. Go back to Step Three, if you see a reason to adjust your action plan."

"Step Five: If necessary, execute those parts of your plan that are not already activated. You've got the framework. You've considered the contingencies. You've determined how to finance it. Now all you have to do is ACT!"

"Step Six is Evaluate and Readjust. Let's suppose that you turned out not to be personally affected by the changes. That is, you're still here, your job may have changed some, but it's roughly equivalent to what you were doing before, or perhaps you've been moved to a different job. Never believe that once it's over, it can't happen again. It can -- and it probably will. *You need to evaluate the process you just went through to see if your networking and strategy were effective or if some changes are required.* Make needed adjustments and rest in the security that you have greater control of your own destiny."

"Suppose you left the company, either because of the downsizing or by choice. Then you still may need to evaluate and readjust the plan for your new line of work. It's hard to find a company of any size where such things aren't happening."

"I don't know what I'd do if that happened to me. I know I'd be hurt."

"That's understandable, Sandra. Be angry or hurt for awhile -- but remember, the best remedy is action. Should you update your skills? Gain others? Retrofit yourself for a new occupation? This is an interesting playing field. *Don't be a spectator.*"

"So what's going to happen to Keli -- and the village?"

"The Elder will be gone for some time. But Keli and Pola and the others will rebuild the village and because of the challenge, they will grow in ability and inner strength. That's what challenges do for us."

"I guess they are some of the tests you spoke of a long time ago."

"They are, Sandra."

"So what's the next chapter about?"

"It's about the rain forest and balance and interdependence."

"Do you have it yet?"

111

"Well, I've got a little bit to go, but here, take the first part and by the time you've finished it, I'll have the rest."

"That's a deal!"

Sandra's Journal

The Ninth Lesson

To survive, assess the potential effect of the change and develop a plan.

To succeed, consider alternatives, develop a strategy and take early action.

The secret is, influence the outcome and its impact on you using your internal and external networks for information, support and help.

> "Nothing is more dangerous than an
> idea,
> When it's the only one we have."
> ...Émile Auguste Chartier

THE TENTH LESSON

On Community

The reorganization was over. Some people -- good people -- were gone. Good-byes had been said. Some were tearful; some, joyful; others full of excitement and hope. There would be retirement for some, new careers for others and some would go back to school or take on other responsibilities. The new PWE organization had been announced and people poured over the charts looking for their names, and the names of their friends. Jack had a new role as Senior Advisor to the President on Employee Issues. Bill had opted for an early retirement package, and Sandra had just told Jack about her promotion to Team Leader in PWE's Wholesale Marketing Division.

"I don't know whether to laugh or cry," she said. "I guess I'd better put on my best face for the new Senior Advisor. An office next to our president -- I'm impressed."

"Frankly, I'll miss it down here on eight. And we'll have a bit of a walk now that you're moving into the Marketing Center. Good exercise for both of us," he grinned. "Have you met with your new team yet?"

"No, but I've heard a few things from their last team leader. It should present an interesting challenge."

"Is there friction?"

113

"No, Jack, nothing as visible as that. From what I hear, it's more like a dysfunctional family, with people going their separate ways. My understanding is -- well, Jack, I think it may be a diversity issue -- but I'm hesitant to say that until I see for myself."

"Good idea not to make any hasty evaluations. PWE and Marketing have made a great choice in you. Have you started Chapter 10?"

"I'm embarrassed, but no. If you'll give me the rest of the chapter, I do have time now."

"Here's a new version," he said reaching into his briefcase. "I've done some serious editing since I gave you the first part. Anyway, I think you'll find it interesting, particularly in view of the challenges you're facing."

She paused at the door, "I'll read it over the weekend. I hope there's some good advice in here, Jack. I have a hunch I'll be needing it."

Saturday afternoon was unusually quiet. Sandra had used all her powers of persuasion to get Steve to run the usual weekend errands alone so she could curl up on the sofa and read. She would pay for it with an extra dose of Sunday afternoon football, he told her. As she picked up the manuscript, she made a mental note to do the wash on Sunday.

The Richness of Diversity

Our group of Gatherers had just returned from a successful five-day expedition with baskets full of the masoesa bush leaves used for cleaning wounds and shemane fern for aching feet. I was looking forward to a few hours of rest and something to eat other than the manioc bread that was a staple on our travels through the jungle. I stopped by the cooking house and helped myself to one of the delicious yams roasting on the fire. There I heard the good news. Bari, one of the Hunters traveling with the Elder, had returned to the village bringing cotton hammocks to replace those lost in the fire. He would be leaving the next morning, so I knew there wasn't much time if I wanted to talk with him. I did not want to miss this opportunity for he had news of the Elder. I found him sitting by the pond with Barto, who was now a Hunter, and had stayed in the village.

When he left the Elder and the others, Bari told us, they were staying with a tribe of Kupas where they had managed to make some very good trades. He had sent a special hammock back for me. I was elated -- first, because the Elder was well and enjoying his travels through the jungle, and second, because I would once again enjoy the comfort of my hammock at night.

There was other news as well. Bari had been accompanied to the village by two members of the Panju tribe, the only survivors of a tribal war. The Elder had befriended them in the jungle where they had shared their provisions and given him items he was able to trade with the Kupas. He had sent them with Bari to become part of our community. The one named Koni was supposed to be expert with a bow and arrow, so he would join the Hunters. The other, Jaro, had worked closely with the Panju Shaman, and the Elder had sent word that he could be a big help to the Healers.

I was not sure how the others would feel about adding a stranger to our group, but I was full of gratitude toward the Elder and decided to do everything in my power to make him welcome. "Where are the Panjus?" I asked. Barto grinned and pointed toward the river.

"Why do you smile?" I asked.

"See for yourself," he snickered.

They were sitting on the river bank when I first saw them. Even from a distance I could see them eyeing me as if I were an unwelcome guest. I raised my hand in greeting. "I am Keli," I said.

They stood up, side by side -- and I was taken aback by the strangeness of their appearance. They were very tall and had feathers in their ear lobes and through their noses as well as strange markings that resembled the caracara hawk painted on their chests. The larger of the two had a

115

string of beads suspended from his lower lip. Their hair was long and coated with a substance that made it glisten in the sunlight. They wore old-fashioned breech cloths of a type no longer used by our tribe. As I approached, the larger one greeted me. "The Elder spoke of you," he said. "I am Koni the Hunter."

Then the other spoke, "I am Jaro," he said. "I do not shoot the bow and arrow as well as my brother. I do know many roots, leaves, and berries. I will work with you and the Healers if they will have me."

For a moment, I hesitated. Then swallowing deeply, I nodded. I wanted to do it -- but the others? Then I turned to Koni. "Where do you sleep?" I asked him.

"There," he said, pointing to a hut about sixty yards from the village. "Come, you will see."

As the three of us walked toward their dwelling, I was struck by how differently we lived. Our houses consisted of light rafters of small palms supported by trunks of forest trees. The roofs were thatched with large leaves neatly arranged and bound to the structure with forest creepers. All our huts were clustered together to form a circle with the chief's hut in the middle. This hut was off by itself. Sticks resting on stilts constituted its main structure. Its roof was made of several layers of palm leaves woven together in a crisscross pattern. A jaguar skin hung across the doorway. Once inside I was even more amazed by how they slept. Instead of the soft swaying hammocks we were used to, they slept on wooden racks.

"Are these comfortable?" I asked.

The brothers grinned. "When we are tired, we sleep," Jaro responded.

As I walked back to the village, I wondered how these strangers would fit into our tribe. Pola, Manu, Mali, Barto and I talked about it as we took our evening walk.

"I don't know how I feel about their being here," said Mali. "They look so fierce with those feathers through their noses and beads hanging from their lips."

"I don't think the Panjus want to fit in," said Manu. "They live away from the village and they even eat by themselves. I'm glad they don't walk the path of the Traders." Manu was now a Trader and had recently returned from the northern village.

"Did you see their hut?" asked Mali. "It looks strange. And Keli says they sleep on wooden racks." She shook her head in disbelief.

"This Koni -- I heard his arrows never miss," said Manu, "and that he can hit a hummingbird in the eye at a distance from here to the river. How do we know they won't get up in the night and attack us? The rest of the Panjus died in a tribal war. We are a peaceful people."

"Wait a minute," said Pola. She had stopped walking and was shaking her head in disapproval. "First of all, the Elder sent Koni and Jaro to live with us. That speaks well for them. In the second place, Manu, since you will be meeting many different people as a Trader I would think you could learn a lot from Koni and Jaro."

"Yes," said Barto. "And don't forget how much they helped us in the jungle. Without their provisions and the trading items, the Elder wouldn't have been able to send back the hammocks and other supplies so quickly."

"Perhaps all will be well," I added. "They seem friendly and eager to be accepted. We could teach them to be more like us. If they give up the breech cloths for our loose-fitting trousers, remove the feathers, and cut their hair...."

"Hold on!" said Pola. "Koni and Jaro are the last survivors of the Panju Tribe. It is right that they should hold to their culture. Perhaps they will teach us about it so we can properly honor them. In our turn, we will teach them about the Korios, *but we should not ask or expect them to take on our ways.*"

"But how will the Panjus adapt to our customs?" I asked.

117

"That is for Koni and Jaro to determine," answered Pola. "*Let us agree that when we speak of either of the brothers that we will not call them the Panjus, which tends to create distance, but rather by the names given them by their parents -- which is what we prefer to be called.*"

I agreed. "That is the respectful thing to do," I said.

"Yes, Keli, and being respectful is only the beginning. No one knows better than you what it feels like to be an outsider. We must include them. Manu, you pointed out that they eat by themselves. If that is their choice, so be it. But I think we have all missed the opportunity to make them welcome by not inviting them to eat with us and walk with us."

"Do we have to?" asked Manu. "What if we don't want to be with strangers?"

"We must not forget, they are part of us now. And *we have much to learn from each other*," said Pola.

"Okay," said Manu. "I'm going to try to make friends with them. But they're going to have to try to fit in."

"Wait a minute, Manu," I said. "*Let's not test our new friends to see if they deserve our friendship.* Jaro worked side by side with the Panju Shaman. That's enough for me. I'll bet he knows some medicines that we have never used."

"I'm going to get some pointers from Koni," said Barto. "I have seen how good he is with a bow and arrow."

In this way, our conversation turned from the fearful, negative view of the Panjus to curiosity and interest in two new members of the tribe, Koni and Jaro. More challenges lay ahead, but we had crossed the first bridge.

"I wish it were that easy to resolve differences," said Sandra, taking another sip of Sprite. She and Jack were sitting in soft blue easy chairs in his new office. "One discussion and all is well."

"I take that as constructive criticism," said Jack. "You're right. ⁚ and his friends have made the first step when they decided not to 'raise the bar,' that is, not to make accepting Koni and Jaro conditional on their conforming to a set of artificial requirements. That's like creating a whole new set of rules for a game in progress. Still, they have a long way to go."

"You made some interesting points, Jack. I laughed when I read about Keli suggesting that Koni and Jaro should give up their feathers and beads in order to be assimilated into the tribe. Then I realized how important it is to differentiate between 'dress codes' and traditions."

"That's right. When it comes to dress codes, every organization has expectations about how its personnel will look and dress. Those are standards. Eliminating diversity is another thing. *That's about attempting to erase traditions and culture in the name of assimilation. It may be well meaning, but it's arrogant. It denies the others' personal worth because what it implies is being different is being deficient,* and it puts them at a disadvantage, sort of like starting a marathon one mile behind everyone else."

Sandra leaned forward. "Jack, one thing really struck home -- when Pola and the others decided to stop referring to the brothers as the Panjus and use their names instead. As I've gone around talking to the members of the team, there have been numerous complaints about 'the Asian.' In fact, T.L. Chin is Taiwanese and clearly doesn't appreciate being lumped with all Asians, as if there's no difference between his culture and that of the People's Republic of China or Japan or Vietnam."

"Can you blame him?" asked Jack. "Don't we, as Americans, see ourselves as quite different from the French or the Germans?"

"Right! and they from us." Sandra leaned forward. *"And calling others by their names, rather than referring to them as part of a group is, as Keli says, giving them the respect they deserve."*

"So, tell me about the complaints you're hearing."

"Well, the team was kept pretty well intact after the downsizing so T.L. is the only new person in the group. I've interviewed each them separately to see what's on their minds. Let me summarize. T say it used to be fun in the team until T.L. showed up. They say he is a workaholic, standoffish, reserved, slow to act, clannish, doesn't mix with the group, and has no sense of humor. Need I go on?"

"Please don't," replied Jack wrinkling his brow. "And what does T.L. say?"

"Well, at first darn little. Finally, I got at it a bit by asking him what his experience as a team member has been like so far."

"And..."

"Well, he sees the team as very cohesive, but he doesn't see himself as a member of it. He says they make fast decisions without thinking them through and they are unwilling to listen. He says he feels tested every single day and that it robs him of energy. And finally, he told me the team does not understand people from Taiwan. Apparently, the first day he came on they decided they would all have dinner together and go out. Without even considering his preferences, they went to their favorite barbecue place. T.L. doesn't eat barbecue. Then they dragged him to a football game. He doesn't like football."

"Neither do you. So much for starting off on the right foot."

"But I give them some credit. They were well-intentioned."

"I wonder how we would feel arriving in Taiwan, only to be treated to a dinner of jellyfish and conversation replete with jokes that made no sense to us," said Jack.

"And, oh by the way, let's complete the picture with a long evening of ritualistic Taiwanese theater that we don't understand."

"Frankly, I think experiencing a different culture would be helpful for all of us. I mean, I know people who travel all over the world so they can hang out with other Americans, eating hamburgers and fries in typical U.S. hotels. But don't get me started. And I do have some ideas that I'd like to bounce off of you, Jack. They're not the answer, but perhaps they are a start."

"I can't wait to hear what you are planning."

"Good, because they include some help from you, not in your official role but as the best mentor anyone could ever have."

"Watch it. When I get that big a compliment, I usually reach in my back pocket and grab hold of my billfold. Seriously, how can I help?"

"Well my plan has three parts to it: first, I think *our group is going to have some teambuilding, and part of that is going to be for each of us to share some things about the history, style and cultural background that have gone into making us unique individuals.* I thought we could develop a listing of all our competencies so we can appreciate the gifts each of us brings and call on each other for help. How's that for a start?"

"I like that. You're not singling T.L. out but opening up the group to disclosing the kind of information that will draw them closer together."

"I think it will help. I'm going to bring in a friend of mine, Charley Jackson, to facilitate the session and help us with the second part, diversity training. Now comes the third part, and if you're willing, you have a part in this."

"You know I'll help if I can," Jack replied.

"I'd like to give T.L. a copy of *Secrets* to read. I want to use it as a coaching tool. He's sharp, and he has some special gifts. He's the only one in the group with a background in international finance. As PWE goes global, we'll need a lot of help working with foreign currency. I don't think we've begun to tap into his expertise. Once the group gets past this hurdle and becomes a team again, and that means that everyone is seen as a contributing member, I think T.L. can teach us all a lot. I know you're busy, but would you be willing to talk with him if he has any questions -- I mean after he's read it. When I think of how much your book helped me -- well, what do you say?"

"Sure, thing," Jack replied, pulling the manuscript from his briefcase. "Anything else I can do?"

Sandra paused and took a deep breath, "Have you got a couple of minutes more?" she asked.

Glancing at his watch, Jack nodded. "I'm in good shape for the next twenty minutes or so."

She stood at the window staring at the skyline for a moment, then turned toward him. "Jack, I'm feeling a bit overwhelmed. I'm not sure I can do a good enough job coaching him."

"Full of self doubts?"

"Yes."

"Do you mind if I ask you a personal question?"

"No."

"Have you ever been discriminated against?"

She nodded as she once again sank down into the warm pillows of the chair. "Yes."

"Do you mind talking about it?"

"Unofficially. Jack, sometimes it's been subtle; sometimes it's been pretty obvious. I've had discounting remarks made to me and heard them made about others in my presence. Sometimes they were made in a joking manner; sometimes I felt there was a serious edge underneath them. I remember going to several meetings with Karen. One of the men made the comment, 'There's Karen and her little shadow.' What a put-down, to be reduced to being a child! I've never heard those kind of comments made to two men who attended together."

"What did you do?"

"Karen and I walked over to him and in a quiet but commanding voice, she said, 'Excuse me, were you talking to me?' He sort of weaseled out. 'I was only kidding. I didn't mean anything by it.' You know the scene. Then she said, 'Have you met Sandra? She's our top performer in Wholesale.' I love the way she handled that, but isn't a shame you have to do such things!"

"It is!" Jack agreed.

"Once I was told that the reason I wasn't asked to be part of a larger meeting was it was a 'men only' session. Now I have no problem with men gathering with other men. I enjoy the company of women too. But Jack, this was a business meeting!"

Jack frowned. "Dinosaurs!" he said.

Sandra sighed. "Some of them were thirty year old dinosaurs, Jack."

"They come in all ages," he said, shaking his head.

"One more thing, Jack. Sometimes discrimination isn't overt. It's not so much what does happen as what doesn't. A case in point: Karen was the best supervisor I've had. She was much smarter and more skilled than any of the managers they brought in over her. I honestly believe she'd have had that job if she'd been a man."

"Why do you say that?"

"I'm not sure, Jack. It's just that the people they brought in spent half their time in her office, seeking her opinion. She came up with all the ideas; they made all the presentations. You tell me."

"Maybe that's one I can look into," said Jack. "Why don't you give me her full name."

"Too late. She took the program. Now she's gotten a great job at Fulmark. That's a loss for PWE."

"Sandra, just a few minutes ago you told me you were worried about coaching T.L. You have nothing to fear. You have a wealth of knowledge and you understand the pain."

"I know, but can I really help him enough?"

"You can, and you will. It's really to your advantage to pull this off. In the world we're living in with a global marketplace out there, being able to leverage off the talents of everyone is an essential skill."

"I know."

"That's only the start of it, Sandra. None of us have a monopoly on good ideas. Think of how much you, the team and ultimately PWE can learn from a different perspective. By the way, it wouldn't hurt to ask T.L. for some ideas on how the team can grow. I'll bet he has given it some thought."

"I'll bet he has."

"Sandra, you spoke of three steps you planned to take. Add one more to your list."

"And that is…"

"*Enabling.* Let's suppose building a network is one of the areas you plan to coach T.L. in. Don't forget that opportunities have to be available. No one can do it sitting in his office, or yours. Sometimes it helps to listen, sometimes to advise, sometimes to encourage, but more than anything, *it helps to find the right occasions so that T.L. can use the coaching.*"

"I need to do that with everyone, don't I?"

"You got it. What do you think are some specific areas where coaching could help."

"There's networking. I know he has close friends who are Taiwanese, and that's great. But he needs to expand his network. I think he's very team-oriented, but at the same time, I want to help him get more recognition for what he contributes. Then there's a more sensitive subject. When I interviewed him, I got the impression that he attributes all issues between him and the team to his being Asian. Many of them really are, but some are typical team disagreements and some are just different business judgments. I'd like to help him focus on doing something about those. I know how easy it is to attribute everything to ethnicity or gender. As a woman, I've fallen into that trap before. The problem is, *it shuts you off from any good feedback and everyone walks on eggshells trying not to offend you which prevents you from growing.*"

"Right!" said Jack. "The team needs to develop a more open and positive communication atmosphere, and you need to set the example."

"Ouch, Jack, you hit a nerve. That's why I'm so overwhelmed. I have no problem giving the others feedback. I'm afraid to give T.L. feedback because of all the sensitivities we've been talking about."

"Don't be. You're good at that. Just be sure it's balanced."

"Balanced?"

"Yes, Sandra. I hope you're telling the whole team, including T.L., what they are doing right. If you can't do that, then you shouldn't tell them how they can improve. Second, don't believe that feedback is your sole prerogative. *If the team is to become totally effective, they all have to take responsibility for feedback.*"

"I know, but that's not where we are now -- not by a long shot."

"Well, there's no doubt you are on the road to building a trusting relationship because you haven't swept this problem under the rug. You're doing something about it. Hopefully the teambuilding and diversity sessions you are planning will open the door to good constructive communication with people giving to and receiving from each other straight, honest and helpful feedback."

He continued, "But let me share an experience I had that could throw a little light on why I feel so strongly about the importance of feedback. Years ago I had an encounter with June, a young African-American who was interning with PWE. She had been assigned to do a report which involved collecting information from me and others. Every one of us found her manner abrasive. Because I didn't know her very well, I thought her supervisor could help her. When I went to see Alice to suggest she might want to coach her or send her to some training on interpersonal skills, she acted surprised, implying no one had ever been critical of June before. Instead of working with her, which I felt was Alice's obligation, she asked me to talk to June. It was awkward because I barely knew her, but I felt she needed to know how she was coming across. Anyway, I did talk with her and she was very grateful. I think it was too late for her with PWE. She didn't receive a offer, and I'll always wonder if it wasn't Alice's fault. Afterwards, several others told me they too had spoken with her about June, even before I did. I was very disappointed in Alice as a PWE manager and I resolved that I would never let such a thing happen again. It was a real loss for PWE. June was bright, creative and had a lot of initiative. We failed her."

"And I'm not going to fail T.L."

"Of course, you're not, Sandra. So, do you mind if I suggest what I think of as six secrets to share with him."

"I've got my pencil out."

"Here are the things you should tell him: *First, seek feedback, because it's information that will help you grow.* If all you hear is positive, keep probing. All of us are imperfect people, being coached by other imperfect people. All of us have room for improvement. Even if you don't like what you hear, don't explain yourself or be defensive. Instead, think about it. If you think it's unfair, try to learn more. People can and do misinterpret our intentions. Information sharing can often put things back in sync. *Above all, don't attribute all feedback to gender or ethnicity. That tends to focus attention on something other than ourselves and prevents us from learning.*"

"*Second, remember no matter how good you are, attitude counts for a lot.*"

"There's a lot of information about attitude in *Secrets*, isn't there?" asked Sandra.

"I hope so," Jack responded. "It's vital for everyone. *People who succeed have the type of attitude that attracts others. They know what's important, and they see themselves as part of the business, not as 'someone doing a job for pay.'* Going the extra mile, being of service, smiling, being cheerful -- all these behaviors draw others to us. Sometimes I'm amazed that people would allow themselves to be negative and disgruntled or arrogant or any of the other behaviors that push people away."

"I guess that includes what we talked about a long time ago. It's not about working harder or longer hours. It's about how you approach work. When you first told me that, I didn't get it. I do now, and it's made a big difference."

"There's a lot of people working long and hard who aren't successful," said Jack leaning forward in his chair. *"You've got to think differently and build your capabilities."*

"Once you said, keep learning. I still am." said Sandra, turning to a fresh page in her notepad. "What's third?"

"It's the golden rule of communication. *If you want others to tune in, you have to be on their wave length.* That means you may need to adjust your volume and alter your speed. Whether you're in a meeting or having a one-on-one conversation, if you want others to listen, don't shout. At the same time, don't speak so quietly that you can't be heard. This is really important. Think about your TV set. If you turn up the volume, everyone holds their ears. If you have it too low, people stop listening. You may need to change the speed too. If people look perplexed, you could be talking too fast. If they look bored, you could be talking too slow. It's like putting a record on a turntable and playing it at the wrong speed. There's a sound and a rhythm to organizational speech. If you can catch on to it, you add to the harmony. If not, well did you ever listen to an orchestra when someone was playing too loud or hit a sour note? It's the same thing."

Sandra nodded. "I guess that's good advice for everybody. I've been guilty of talking too slow. Sometimes I've used more air time than I should. But don't listeners have obligations too."

"They do, but we both know there's a natural tendency for our minds to wander when we aren't fully engaged."

"That happens to me sometimes," said Sandra.

"I can take a hint," Jack laughed, "so let's move on. Fourth *important to join with others, but don't give up being who you the name of being accepted.* In a symphony orchestra, the cell oboe is called on to solo because it has special qualities. Don't downplay yours."

"Next, *if you have to choose between being loved and being respected, go for respect.* The big difference is, *love is freely given, but respect is earned.* What I'm saying, Sandra, is this. I've seen people put up with offensive jokes or innuendoes and laugh along with everyone else just to gain the 'love' of the group. Every time you do that, you lower your self esteem, and you set yourself up for the next time. This doesn't encourage others to modify their behavior because they believe what they are saying or doing doesn't bother you. If someone else says the comment was offensive, the person merely points to the fact that you thought it was funny too. Obviously there are a choice of remedies -- everything from walking away, providing feedback or taking your concerns higher if necessary. *Whatever you choose, do something, but do it with dignity.*"

"Sixth, when things go well for you, *don't abandon the others* who could use a hand up. That's my list. I imagine others might have a different one." Glancing at his watch, Jack stood up. "Speaking of talking too much…."

Sandra knew the discussion was over. "I can see my twenty minutes are about up. I like your list, and I think T.L. will too. You talk about giving others a hand up. That's one thing I appreciate about you, Jack. You're always there to lend a hand." With a smile, she was gone.

*   *   *

And Laura was gone too. She was off to the ballet with two close friends, leaving Jack on his own for the evening. He settled in his favorite easy chair with a book. After thirty minutes he realized that he had seen words and turned pages, but he couldn't remember what he had read. He was restless. Walking to the bookcase, he picked up a ook about the rain forest. As he looked at the pictures, his thoughts ted to his discussion with Sandra, to T.L. and to the beauty of the forest where over 3,000 different tree species thrive side by side. as diversity! He put down the book and moving to his desk n the computer. It could be a long night.

The next morning Sandra found a brown envelope on her desk. It contained this note from Jack. "More on Chapter 10. Let me know what you think." She picked up the manuscript and read.

Jaro and I had spent the morning walking through the jungle with each of us pointing out the uses of particular berries, roots, plants and fungi. I was delighted at his level of knowledge for I had thought the Panjus a more primitive people based on Koni and Jaro's appearance. I now understood what a mistake that was. Jaro had an inquisitive nature that he attributed to his culture. Just yesterday, he had taught me a method developed by the Panjus for preparing ointments that was far superior to any I had ever seen. Jaro confessed that he too had drawn some assumptions based on the Korios "modern" dress. He had assumed that we had lost the old knowledge of medicines and was pleased to learn this wasn't so.

We stopped to rest and ate the sweet hogplum fruit we had picked earlier and wrapped in our bandannas. The silence was broken by the screech of a piha bird in the tree beside which Jaro was seated. We looked up. Spotlighted by narrow shafts of light, the tree was a circle of energy alive with brightly-colored birds, tree frogs and monkeys. Yet, I knew as tall as the tree was, the part of its roots beneath the jungle floor were probably buried no deeper than the length of my arm. It was the lianas, huge vines that wrapped themselves around the tree on their climb toward the sun, that held it firmly to the ground. The fungi that lived on the tree roots nourished the tree. The insects of the jungle fed from the fungi, which helped feed the seeds of the beautiful flowers that lived atop the branches, creating beauty and drawing life from the tree. And the small animals of the jungle spread the life of the tree by dropping its seeds and fruit in new places.

The tree, with its strength and beauty, might appear to stand on its own, but without the various gifts brought to it by the lianas, the fungi, the birds, the animals, it would die. There was life in the jungle; there was death too, but the gifts that nourished the tree came from many different places -- all varied, all beautiful, all one.

I looked over at Jaro and wondered if he had seen this too. He smi'

Sandra's Journal

The Tenth Lesson

To survive, treat everyone you work with as a worthy business partner.

To succeed, give helpful feedback to others and ask others to give you feedback.

The secret is, we all profit when we actively invite diverse perspectives and encourage free interchange of ideas.

THE ELEVENTH LESSON

On Direction and Purpose

Leaning back in his chair, his legs sprawled out in front of him, Jack clasped his hands behind his neck and yawned. He gazed out of the window watching the lights of the city just coming on. They sparkled against the evening sky. Winter! Thanksgiving was not far off. And then....

"I know you're not busy," she said softly. She was standing in the doorway holding two steaming cups in one hand and her briefcase in the other.

"Come on in, Sandra," he laughed. "You caught me daydreaming."

"Look outside. It's more like nightdreaming right now. Jack, I hate to disturb you, but I had to talk to you. I called Francine and she said you were still here. She gave me the tea. Said you enjoy it at the end of the day."

131

"Francine's a jewel, and she knows I can get my own."

"She told me you'd complain. But I said, never mind him. Anyway, T.L. read *Secrets* and likes it a lot. He's made notes on the things he found most useful, and we've been discussing some enabling ideas that will help him increase his network."

"That's great, but I sense there's more or you wouldn't be here at six o'clock. Steve making supper?"

"No, although he cooks more than I do. We're going out tonight. I know how busy you are, but I have a request from T.L. and I thought I should make it in person. Jack, he feels since you mention *purpose* in a number of places, the book should provide some help in this direction. Do you know what I mean?"

"I think so. You're saying T.L. wonders how you know what your purpose is, right?"

"I guess that's it. To put a little meat around the bare bones, he's asking 'How far do I want to go in my career, and how much am I prepared to sacrifice to get there?' I'd add to that some questions I've had from time to time, like how do you manage your business life so that you still have a personal life? Is your work supplementary to your life or vice versa? Anyway, I promised T.L. I would bring it up. Now I have to go."

He stood up and put on his jacket. "Me too. I just need to put a few things away and I'm out of here. Laura's got dinner on the stove and she cooks a mean spaghetti. Sandra, I'm glad you stopped by. Those are good questions, and I'll have to give them some serious thought. If you wanted to put me back to work on the book, you've succeeded. I've been away from *Secrets* too long. Time I finished it."

She picked up her briefcase. "Say hello to Laura."

"Go! Enjoy your dinner. My best to Steve. I'll call."

The call came ten days later. By then, the brown envelope had een delivered, opened, and read. Keli's story continued…

Purpose

It was several years before I saw the Elder again. When he finally returned from his travels, he brought with him Yna, a Kupan woman he had taken for a wife. We had rebuilt the village long before he came back, and thus they were able to stay in my house while Manu, Barto and I built a new dwelling to replace the one destroyed in the fire. In those first few weeks, there were few opportunities to talk alone. He was much in demand, for all wanted to hear about the far off places he had been to and the strange things he had seen. Everyone in the village drew upon his wisdom, and so some time went by before we climbed the hill together.

I was looking forward to our time alone for I knew we would have much to talk about, and yet with the passing of years, I sensed a difference in our relationship. He was still like a father to me, but I was no longer a child. When we met early that morning, it was I who led the way and I who brought the cassavas and smoked capybara meat we would share. As we sat together once again enjoying the peacefulness of the hill, it was he that broke the silence.

"You have found your purpose, Keli."

"How did you know that?"

"Your eyes reveal your inner satisfaction. That only comes when you have made your choice."

"Father, after you left, I spent some time with the Hunters. I traveled with Koni and the others through the deepest jungle to places where the only relief from darkness was the slender rays of sunlight that filtered through the tree tops. It was a great adventure and I wanted to do it, but I came to understand, it would not be my future. For several months I worked with Lutar and Tani helping them carve blowguns and bows from the spotted snakewood tree and make knives from peccary jaws. When the months had passed, I had renewed admiration for the Toolmakers, but I knew this was not the end of my search. I then went down the river with Manu, Kodi and the other Traders. I enjoyed it a lot, but I was restless to return to the village. It was on this trip that I became fully aware of what I wanted to do and to be."

"And what was that, my son?"

"I wanted to stay a Healer, to teach and counsel others as you have taught and counseled me. I wanted to do these things, but I knew I wasn't ready. I needed to learn more about the mysteries of the jungle. How would I acquire this knowledge? I could not draw upon your wisdom, for you were off on your travels. After some searching, I went to the Shaman and asked if he would allow me to learn under his teaching -- to be his helper."

"That was a good solution. And what was his answer?"

"He thought about it for nine days. On the tenth day, he asked me to walk with him."

"And?"

"He asked me how I made this decision."

"And how did you?"

"It started on the day we met when I finally admitted to myself that I was lost. It took me some time to understand that experience for at the time I believed the most important thing in my life was to fit in. You helped me up and told me then that I needed to dedicate myself to learning if I wanted to find the path that leads to true contribution. *What I came to understand is that path is different for everyone.*"

"*That is true, my son, for each of us has his own gifts to share.*"

"Later, when I was satisfied to stay in my role as a Sorter, you sensed my fear of losing my place in the tribe, and you encouraged me to move on. *You told me I was on a journey, and you helped me see if I wanted to find my purpose I should listen to my thoughts, examine my heart and be guided by what they told me.*"

"*Yes, that's true, for no one can find a purpose for another.*"

"I thought many times about what was important to me, and I realized I was searching for something to give my life direction. My journey began when I got over my fears of not belonging. Thank you, Father, for helping me to understand that. It continued as I struggled to find my own way when you left after the fire and I found my greatest satisfaction was in helping others. But even then, I wasn't sure. That is why I chose to walk through the jungle beside the Hunters, work with the Toolmakers, and travel with the Traders."

"Then you learned that following those paths was wrong for you."

"I did. But I also learned some other things. For when I walked with the Hunters, I discovered how greatly they valued my knowledge of medications. I found myself advising them about various ointments and balms. I made them salves they could put on their feet to take out the soreness; I prepared a treatment for their rashes. For me, that was the best part of the hunt."

"Was it also so when you worked with the Toolmakers and the Traders?"

"It was. That was where my satisfaction came from, from being of service. But how should I do it? Then I remembered something you told me."

"And that was..."

"You told me if I shot an arrow, I would know when it found the mark. So when I came back from my Trading expedition and before I returned to the Healers, I spent some time thinking about exactly what I wanted to do. I had been a Sorter. It was an interesting part of my education, but that was over. I had enjoyed Gathering for it enabled me to see many parts of the jungle, but I didn't want to go back to that."

"Aren't they all of service?"

"They are. But I wanted to do more, to learn more, to be more."

"When you spoke to the Shaman, were you aware of how much sacrifice might be required of you?"

"I was. And that was the conflict I had to resolve. I spoke to Mali about this. You may not know, Father, but she and I are promised."

"I knew. I'm happy for you both. What did she tell you?"

"She will wait for me."

"How long will that be?"

"The Shaman tells me if he accepts me, it will be two years."

There were tears in his eyes. "He will accept you. We have spoken."

Jack smiled as he said good morning to Francine, but his heart wasn't in it. The old Packard had been acting up again and he was exasperated. "That's it!" he thought. "One more major repair job. If that doesn't do it, Laura and I will look at cars. No more roaming the street. The old boy will have to be satisfied spending the rest of his life on blocks in my garage."

With a piece of paper in her hand, Francine followed him in to his office. "My goodness, you're in a hurry today. You walked by so fast I didn't have time to give this to you."

"Please accept my apologies. I've let the old crate make me late for the last time." He glanced at the sheet in his hand. It contained a diagram with a note on the bottom.

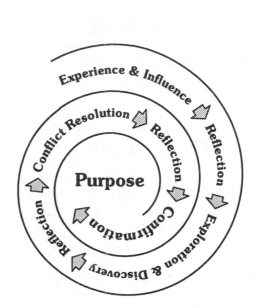

The note read, "T.L. put this together after reading Chapter 11. He describes it as the process of understanding one's purpose. He thought you might want to put it in your book if it makes sense. Francine says you have some time to talk at two thirty. See you then. Sandra. P.S. I invited T.L. to come along. Hope you don't mind."

Jack didn't mind at all. The morning would be filled with budget meetings. By two thirty he would welcome the chance to meet with Sandra and T.L. and talk about the book. Besides, he had something important to discuss with Sandra. He wondered how she would react to the news? Maybe this was the wrong time to talk about it. But when is the right time?

Jack was pacing when Sandra and T.L. knocked on the door. "Today's the day," he said aloud. Instantly he felt better as he walked to the door.

As she came in with T.L., Sandra pretended to look around. "There must be someone behind the curtains. I heard you talking." She grinned. "Things must be pretty bad when you're talking to yourself."

"I was, and they're not. Hi T.L., what did you bring this nosy lady up here for?" he asked. Everyone laughed. "I thought your diagram captured the essence of the process, T.L. and with your permission, I'll use it. I'd like to credit your work in the book."

T.L. smiled. "With pleasure. I like models. They help me focus. I'm interested in the subject of finding my purpose, and I was hoping we could talk about it some more today. Also, I have some questions for you, Jack."

"I like it too," added Sandra. "It's typical of the high quality work T.L. does and his insight. And, Jack, I liked your description of how Keli came to understand his purpose. It certainly has been true of my experience."

"And mine," Jack said, nodding his head in agreement. "T.L., I'll be glad to talk about the subject, and answer your questions, if I can. The way I see it, finding your purpose is a journey to self-discovery. It involves a process that alternates times of action with times of reflection. The journey can begin in many different ways. It can come from a great personal hurt or success, key events, or perhaps from someone who inspires or influences us. The point is, we set out deliberately at some point to understand the meaning of these influences and experiences."

"So, what you're saying is having these experiences or influences is not enough. You have to take the time to think about the implications. Isn't that it?" asked T.L.

"That's vital. Otherwise you just go on to the next experience. That's how so many people live their lives, as part of a series of discreet activities and experiences."

"That's why it was important in the story that Keli reflect on his experiences and look for patterns that shaped his reaction to them," added Sandra. "He must ask himself how they fit together. Where do the 'arrows' hit? What are the messages for him? Right so far?"

"That's it, Sandra."

"Even then he should continue exploring, shouldn't he?" asked T.L. "Isn't that why Keli joined the Hunters and the Toolmakers for a while? Wasn't he testing his purpose to make sure he had made the right choice?"

Jack nodded. "That's the way I see it."

"But what happens if you aren't sure, even after you have explored other things?" asked T.L.

"Keep exploring," said Jack. "Some people never find their purpose because they don't take the time to look for it. They are satisfied to 'keep on keeping on.' Others are so eager to find their purpose that they stop too soon, and settle for something less than satisfying. Some people are influenced by others. They want to be just like their dads or their mothers. They wind up trying to live someone else's dream and wind up disappointed with their lives. *The point is, something rings true for you. What is it? Each person must discover that for himself.*"

"Why can't someone else help you decide?" asked T.L. "There are important people in my life who want to be part of the decision. In my culture, we are devoted to our families."

"They are the influences that help to shape your experience. And they need to be considered and involved. So don't leave them out. What I'm really talking about is people who let others make these decisions or don't think of purpose at all. I see them as outer-directed. The problem is, being outer-directed fosters dependency and a continuous need for approval. That means others can control them, and that keeps them weak and powerless. To build enough confidence and self-esteem to handle the important decisions of life, you must be inner-directed. That means you are responsible and accountable for the decisions you make. If they are good ones for you, then you take the credit. If they don't turn out the way you want them to, then you accept the consequences. Let's suppose you decide your purpose in life is to be the ideal son. That's up to you. What I'm suggesting is, if that's your purpose choose it wholeheartedly. Seeing it as a sacrifice takes the joy out of it. In some sense, we make others pay when we make them responsible for our choices."

T. L. nodded. "That makes sense. I think I understand the process. What would help me is a real life example." He turned to Jack.

"I guess I'm elected," said Jack. "It's kind of a long story, but let's start with the big picture. Over the years I've come to realize that each of us has our own special gifts. One óf mine is the ability to explain abstract concepts in concrete ways using examples, metaphors and stories. This 'gift' has helped me explain the source of problems, come up with creative solutions and generate enthusiastic support from others. Now I have three abiding interests in life: I enjoy people, business and the outdoors. One of the values I've received from working at PWE is the opportunity to combine all three into a satisfying career."

"Over time I've come to realize my purpose: in order to succeed, people have to understand this business that is life and this life that is business. I see my purpose as helping with the latter."

"How did you come to know this was your purpose?" asked T.L.

"The model you drew explains the process. Of course, it's never quite as neat as that. Through scouting I developed a love for the outdoors -- backpacking, camping and fishing. When I was still a teenager I went rock climbing with a group in South America. In my last couple of years at high school, I spent the summer doing volunteer work in national forests. Several times I helped build natural barriers to stop the spread of forest fires. I learned a lot about myself in those years. I learned to love and respect nature. I learned that I enjoyed working with others to overcome difficulties. I got a lot of satisfaction from contributing to something bigger than myself."

"I wonder why you didn't make your career in the outdoors," mused T.L.

"I was leaning in that direction," said Jack. "I took a year off from college to travel around. During that period I thought a lot about what I wanted to do with my life. Part of the time I spent in the rain forests of South America with my roommate, a biology major, who wanted to work for a pharmaceutical company doing research. As it turned out, he went to work for PWE. I wasn't interested in research. I found it too analytical and removed from the excitement. When I returned from my trip, I spoke to a professor, who had been a mentor to me from the beginning and was a man I greatly admired. He suggested a career in marketing. At first, I equated that with being a 'traveling salesman' but he was able to paint pictures of marketing careers in larger companies, particularly those in the food or coffee business that sounded more like what I wanted, an opportunity to travel, meet new people, be on the front lines. But he also told me if I was to compete, I needed an MBA. So, I stayed in school."

"When I graduated, I went to work for Reed and Connors, a competitor of PWE that specialized in brokering fruits. With R&C I thought I would be able to work with many different people, travel and enjoy the outdoors too. I was wrong. The first thing they did was put me in an accounting-type job. I was in an office all day, and I had little interaction with people. It was then that I realized how much I needed to work with and around people, so they put me into a retail business But there, I was basically cooped up all day working with groceries and dealing with paperwork half of the night. I thought about my situation quite a bit, but I didn't want to leave the company -- not at first. Laura and I had married, and we were expecting our first child. So, job security was important. I kept hearing how things would get better. They didn't. But R&C was a pretty closed company, and even though I let my supervisor know a number of times how dissatisfied I was, all I got back were platitudes and promises. I thought about my options for a long time before I made my move. Go for security or go for satisfaction. Laura and I talked about it many times. I decided to go for both, with satisfaction being the more important."

"After seven years I left R&C to work for Janek Markets, a small wholesale grocery chain operating in third world countries. That was a fun period of my life. Because Janek was small, I was able to do many different jobs there at the same time. What I realized was, I loved being part of the business decisions that helped the company flourish. I still traveled and saw many interesting parts of the world, but that part of it was not as fulfilling as developing employees was. I still had my interests in the out of doors, but I was able to enjoy that on the weekends. Laura is quite a nature lover and we traveled during the summers as well as occasionally at work."

"So why did you leave Janek?" asked T.L.

"I didn't. It left me. You see, when Janek became highly profitable, it was noticed by many other companies -- in particular, R&C. I didn't want to be part of that company again. I never felt their philosophy compatible with mine, so as work on the merger began, I started looking around. That's when I got in touch with Dave Goldman, my former roommate. Sure enough, he was still happily at work with PWE Pharmaceuticals. With his help and support, I was hired into the Food Division, where I developed my specialty in coffee. For a number of years I traded in the Andes, living part of my career here and part in that region of the world."

"During my tenure at PWE, I've had some jobs I greatly enjoyed and some I didn't care for as much -- but even so, this is a great company. Four years ago, Hal Asher who was Senior Veep in charge of Human Relations asked me if I would leave Marketing and work with Bill Jameson to set up a company-wide HR mentoring program. It was through that assignment that two things happened: first, I came to realize that mentoring is not a program but a relationship built between two people, and second it confirmed my earlier belief that what I loved most was helping people develop. So I stayed in the Human Resources organization working with Controller's, Treasurer's and Marketing. The more I did this, the more I realized how many people there are out there who don't understand the way organizations work or how to be successful in today's world. Hence the book. So, T.L., if you thought that I started the book because I love writing, you'd be wrong. I started the book because I love to explain organizations to people and because I am personally invested in their understanding the life that is business. And, I used the metaphor of the jungle not only because I've been there, but also because I love the mystery and the secrets it represents."

T.L. nodded. "I think that's a wonderful story, Jack. You should put it in your book."

Jack smiled. "Maybe the next one. This is Keli's story. With your model, people should be able to get the main ideas."

T.L. turned to Sandra. "Have you found your purpose?"

142

"Yes," said Sandra. "It's taken me many experiences and a whole lot of introspection to be sure of what is important to me. Jack has played an essential role in this. What I want is to inspire others to take responsibility for their lives. That's really why I see this concept of knowing what you want as so important."

"But how does your job enable you to do that?" asked T.L.

Sandra smiled. "It enables me to help others the way Jack helped me. Coaching and mentoring give me an opportunity to live my purpose. It's like passing on the joy of living to another person. The more I think about it, the more sure I am of one thing -- if I couldn't find true satisfaction in my work, I'd have to leave it. And that would create a real problem for me because PWE is a great company."

"That's one of the things I tried to bring out in Keli's story," said Jack. "Life is full of choices, all competing for our time and energy. The beauty of purpose is that it helps us resolve these conflicts. which, in turn, has a positive effect on our self-esteem and makes us better able to deal with larger problems."

"Well Keli was fortunate," noted T.L. "Mali is willing to wait two years and to go along with his decision to study with the Shaman."

"True," replied Jack. "I suppose if she had refused, he would have to reconsider his purpose and determine what he wants to do. That might call for repeating the process in terms of, exploring how he truly feels, and determining what's most important to him. The key is, if he gives up his dream to make her happy, he will probably be sorry and may resent her. That will add too much baggage to their relationship, and they might not be truly happy. On the other hand, if he were to choose to marry Mali now rather than learn under the Shaman in that scenario, he should enter into it gladly because that's what is most important to him."

"Can't he do both?" asked T.L.

"Not in *Secrets*. He must make a choice. In the real world, many people opt for both. It's usually a continuous struggle of shifting priorities until they decide what takes precedence. When you can't decide, well, that's where negative stress comes from."

"I know you consider finding your purpose a key to the story," said T.L. "Could you tell me why -- in a nutshell."

"Well, I've already said that purpose helps us make choices," said Jack. "But there's more. It's what sets us apart. Look at the people who are successful at PWE. *They have a sense of what they believe and what they want. Purpose helps us gain the respect of ourselves and others and increases confidence in our own judgment.* It helps us manage our time and life better, because we know what is important. There are so many pulls and tugs in life today, without purpose we can lose ourselves in a flurry of meaningless activities."

"Like I do sometimes when I wonder what happened to the day and what I accomplished," added Sandra. "If I stop then and refocus on what has meaning for me and/or what is most important, I feel more in control."

"Right on!" said Jack. "I know people who put their total effort into their career for six months at a time and wonder why they don't have a life."

"Or people who are constantly changing their minds because they don't know what they want," added T.L.

Sandra nodded in agreement. "I read about a woman who said her goal at work was to keep busy. That's all, just keep busy. The reporter thought that was great. Busy doing what? I felt sorry for her because she was activity driven."

"And outer-directed," added Jack.

"Speaking of busy, we've taken enough of your time, Jack. But if you can spare it, I need a minute or two alone with you."

T.L. and Jack shook hands as Jack ushered him out and closed the door. "What's up?"

"Jack, I'm excited. Do I have news for you!"

"I have news too. You go first."

"I've been promoted. It won't be announced till next week, but you're looking at the new Section Head over Retail Sales. I have so many plans, so many things I'd like to go over with you."

"Congratulations," he said. "I'm proud of you."

"I guess I'm kind of like Keli. I look back and see all the things you've done for me, and..."

"Now don't get teary on me," said Jack swallowing hard. "I have some news too. I'm taking early retirement from PWE, Sandra. I'll be leaving the end of next month."

The tears. He could see them welling up in her eyes. "How will I ever get along without you, Jack. You've been like..."

"Don't you dare say 'like a Father to me'," he smiled. "And don't cry or I'll cry too."

There was a long silence during which Sandra fiddled with her purse. Then she looked up. "What brought this on? What will you do?"

"Writing the chapter on 'purpose' helped. I've been pulled so many ways. I want to write, but I've been so busy. Now I've got a publisher, and..."

She broke out in a wide smile. "Whoopee. You're going on a book tour, aren't you?"

"Looks that way. Laura and I will have time to spend together, and I will, of course, keep in touch." He walked to his desk and from behind it brought out a box, gift wrapped with a red ribbon on top. "Here, Sandra. I want you to have this."

"But what's the occasion?" she asked.

"Call it a celebration gift. When I saw this at the store, I thought of you. From what I gather, you are highly thought of at PWE, and the future looks good. I'm very proud of you, Sandra."

"Jack, this isn't fair. It is I who should be giving you a gift. You're the one who is retiring."

"If you want to give me a gift, promise me this…that you will pass on the secrets I have shared with you to others who long for success and aren't sure of the way. There are many of them out there, and all they need is someone like you to point them in the right direction."

"I promise."

"And Sandra, do remember how important Steve is in your life. Carve out more time for him. It pays big dividends."

"Always my teacher."

"Always your friend."

It was later that week when Sandra put the next entry in her journal.

Sandra's Journal

The Eleventh Lesson

To survive, know your purpose and use it to set priorities and to make choices in your life.
To succeed, make sure your work relates to your purpose and makes a difference in the organization.
The secret is, knowing your purpose and being inner-directed makes you better able to unravel the mysteries of the jungle for yourself and others.

> "A teacher affects eternity; he can
> never tell where his influence stops."
> ...Henry Brooks Adams

THE TWELFTH LESSON

On Becoming a Mentor

"Dear Jack,

"I'm speechless -- well almost. As you know, I'm never really speechless. What a wonderful surprise to come to the office today and find a package from you sitting in the middle of my desk. The book is wonderful. I mean, after reading the manuscript and everything, it is so exciting to see a real book waiting for me -- and a letter from you to boot. You've made my day. Are you planning a sequel? I know Keli will complete his education with the Shaman and marry Mali, so I guess his future is set. Still, I am sure there are so many other stories you could tell about the organizational jungle.

"It sounds like you have had great fun on the book tour. So now you're off to the Greek Islands on vacation. How I envy you. But I'm happy for you and Laura. In answer to your question, yes I am holding up PWE just fine, though I miss our long talks. It's hard to believe it has been nine months since you left. And yes, I am keeping my promise. How could I not?

"Do you remember Marsha Nichols? She's the young accountant that works for Dan Chambers, the Tax Attorney down the hall from me. Dan's pretty gruff, but he has the legendary heart of gold. I had gotten the impression that he was not all that happy with Marsha, but I suspected it was a personality conflict more than a performance issue. Anyway, one day a few months ago I was sitting in my office working on the agenda for a meeting when I heard loud voices in the

147

hall right outside my office. (You don't know how many times I have regretted having an office so close to the coffee room.) Anyway, I got up to close the door just in time to see Marsha hurrying away. Billie Roger, Dan's paralegal, was standing there, hands on hips.

"'Excuse the commotion, Sandra,' she said. 'I know we must have disturbed you. I just can't get along with that woman. She's got a problem with her mouth and a chip on her shoulder that's too big for me to knock off. No wonder she eats lunch alone.' (Billie always did have a gift for words.)

"I told Billie I was sorry she and Marsha were having problems and, mumbling a couple of other pat phrases, managed to shut the door before she could say much more. When Billie feels offended, she can go on and on, if you know what I mean. Anyway, about an hour later I heard a tap on my door -- just one tap, mind you. When I opened it, there was no one there, but I saw Marsha walking toward the coffee room. Now, I remembered you had a role in recruiting her and thought a lot of her, and I was curious about what she might have wanted, so I grabbed my cup and followed her in there to see if I could find out. I really wasn't sure how she would react if I asked her why she had knocked and walked away. Marsha has built quite a reputation. Did you know that? In the year she has been on our floor, she has become known as an aggressive, combative loner. But there in the coffee room, she didn't look like she wanted to fight. In fact, I recognized the same lost expression on her face you must have seen from across your desk when you looked at mine several years ago. 'Marsha, was that you at my door?' I asked her.

"She blushed. 'Yes. But I decided not to disturb you.'

"I told her I was taking a break for some coffee and invited her to my office. For a short time, we sat across the desk from each other in silence. Finally Marsha spoke. 'You're a friend of Jack's, aren't you?'

"'A good friend,' I told her.

"'He's always been such a nice man. I'm sorry he left. If you hear from him, would you please tell him I said hello.' I nodded, and she started to leave, but I had a feeling she had not said what she wanted to say.

"'Don't leave yet, Marsha,' I said. 'Tell me, how are things going for you?'

"She sighed, 'Not well. I guess you heard the noise in the hall. You would have had to be unconscious not to hear it. Billie and I were going at it again. At least we speak. That's more than I get from most people here. Except you, Sandra. You've been friendly from the first and I appreciate it. Anyway, I'm really sorry we disturbed you. That's what I came to say.'

"'I'm sorry things aren't going well for you at PWE, Marsha,' I said. 'Jack used to sing your praises. He said you were intelligent, articulate and a real leader in school. That's why PWE worked so hard to recruit you.

"'Really. I wish he'd have told that to Dan. I get the impression he doesn't see it that way.'

"'I'm sorry,' I said. 'I know how hard it is to work when you don't feel appreciated. How long have you been here?'

"'At PWE, three years. Working for Dan Chambers, eleven months. Ask me how long I'm staying. That may be a better question.'

"'How long is that?' I asked.

"'I'm not sure. I don't even know why I said that. It's not like I haven't thought about leaving. Somehow, this place -- I don't have any friends. I don't fit in. It's like everyone else is playing off one sheet of music and I'm playing off another.'

"In that moment I wondered how many lost souls roam our halls and the halls of other organizations in this country. And Jack, I understood why you asked me to make that promise. You've left me to carry on in your place, haven't you? That's fine, because I'll keep that commitment with pleasure. That day I told Marsha a story -- about torches and lamps. I've been mentoring her for the last two months using your manuscript because I didn't have the book. We're up to Chapter Five.

This afternoon I'm going to surprise her with her own copy, and I'm going to buy three or four more copies to keep in my desk. There are other Marshas and Sandras and Kelis out there. Of that, I am sure. What I never realized was how much satisfaction there is in helping another person. I think you can tell, I'm hooked.

"But Jack, you know me. I like to be thorough, like you. So I decided if I was going to be half the mentor you've been, I would need to be sure I had the qualities it takes. I have made a list of them. I might add I determined what the qualities should be by watching you in action. I'd love to know what you'd put on the list, but here's my seven, in no particular order.

"I think *one thing a mentor needs is a genuine interest in others.* I have known people who never smile, never take a moment to say hello. You meet them in the hall and they ask you how you are feeling and keep on walking. They seem too preoccupied to care. People like that don't know what they're missing. From the very first, I felt you cared about me. I knew you were someone I could confide in, someone who would really listen without making me feel foolish, and I was sure you sincerely wanted to help.

"*The second quality is empathy.* It's one thing to care but to truly understand how another feels, that's special. I was the one with the problems, but you had a way of accepting my feelings, of seeing the world from my point of view. I knew there were times you didn't agree with me, and that was helpful too. Whether I was furious about my performance appraisal or confused about moving into the marketing job, I felt understood.

"*Third is perspective.* How we all seem to lose our sense of proportion when it comes to our own problems! I know I did. It was your gift to help me look beyond the immediate moment and even past my own interests to broader issues. I remember when we talked about the five levels of commitment, and I realized how stuck I was in my own world. I was doing my own tasks and wondering why I wasn't appreciated. You made me realize I was Sandra, Inc., and part of a larger enterprise. I asked you then which level of commitment you identified with me but you had the wisdom and the objectivity to let me be the judge.

That was powerful. I admire you for that, and it's one quality I'm going to work hard to emulate. So good mentors share their perspectives, but they don't make judgments.

"Fourth is balance. I'm sure I would have preferred at times that you totally agree with me, but you helped me see situations from both sides. Was I overreacting? Was there a lesson for me? Only a true friend can do that. I can tell you first hand, it's easy to fall into the trap of becoming an advocate. But that doesn't help the other person. Balance is a particular challenge for me with Marsha. She's had a couple of 'challenging' supervisors, and it's a continuing struggle to help her understand how much her defensiveness contributes to the problems she has. She's coming around, though. She's been getting some praise from Dan lately, and she and Billie have started going to lunch. I think I see some daylight here.

"Fifth is the willingness to openly admit our own mistakes. When I came to you with problems, it helped me a lot when you let me know you had been there. I probably would not have been as willing a learner if you had preached from a lofty pedestal. But you never did, Jack. One of the roles of a mentor, I think, is to share our own struggles. When I got that mediocre performance review from Bill, I was devastated. What helped me most is when you told me of a similar situation from your past. I thought, 'Jack overcame this; so can I.'

"Because you were successful, I had confidence in your advice. That's the sixth quality and an essential one. I guess you can call it credibility. Once I asked you if mentors were really necessary. You explained things using a golf analogy. You said, 'If you want to learn the game, you can hit a million balls at the driving range or you can take lessons from a pro.' You're a pro, Jack and if I hadn't seen you as one, I would not have placed such high value on your counsel. I think that's important to anyone who relies on another for advice. Apparently, Marsha sees me that way. I only hope I'm worthy of her trust.

"Finally, a good mentor absolutely must have a sense of humor. So much of what goes on in an organization is deadly serious. Whether it's being in the midst of a downsizing or struggling through turf problems, you have to help people see the light side. Why? Because it's

hard to find creative solutions or take positive actions when you're filled with gloom. Remember when Bill told me to 'lighten up?' I really think I did, thanks to you. You had a way of putting things in perspective -- of seeing the humor in situations and helping me see it too.

"So there's my list of seven. I may think of more later on, but if I get these down I'll have it made. I keep the list in my lap drawer. And I'm working to improve in all those areas.

"Now, let me respond to your other questions. First, about T.L. He's doing great. He was a real asset to our team. Yes, Jack, I said 'was.' It seems you can't hold on to someone with his talent. He's moved on to Treasury Coordination, where his analytical skills and expertise in foreign exchange have Mel Ashton grinning from ear to ear. Why not? He'd make any manager look good. The team misses him. We gave him a great going away party. He chose the restaurant -- guess where -- Alfredo's. Isn't that one of your favorite restaurants too? We all spent the evening eating spaghetti and listening to Italian tenors sing opera. What a fun night that was!

"Oh, and you asked for a copy of my journal, so here it is. The original sits on the small table in my office next to your lovely gift.

"Thank you for being the most wonderful mentor anyone could ever have. I know you're in the big leagues now, with your book and all, but Steve and I would love to have you and Laura come to dinner when you get back from Greece. Please give us a call.

"Hugs to Laura,

"Sandra"

Carefully, she folded the letter and sealed the envelope placing it on the table next to the beautiful porcelain lamp Jack had given her that day he told her he was leaving. Sandra had kept it and the journal in her office as a constant reminder of her promise. She picked up *Secrets* admiring the dust cover, a simple drawing of an ocelot sitting on a branch, its head half hidden by leaves. Just like the mysteries of the jungle, she thought. She opened the book and smiled. Then her eyes filled with tears. There would be one last journal entry after all.

Sandra's Journal

The Twelfth Lesson

Beneath the heading, she copied the dedication from _Secrets of the Jungle:_

"To Sandra, a lamp whose light radiates wherever she goes. Here is the greatest secret. Remember it, and share it with others: if you would be successful, think of all the things you prize and willingly bestow them on another; if you want trust, trust others; if you want credit, give it to others; if you want praise, praise others; if you want love, then love others. Yours is the legacy of the lamp. Keep shining. Your friend, Jack."

Index

K

Korio 26
Korios 13, 26, 40, 82, 117, 129
Kupan 133
Kupas 115

L

Lamp 10, 11, 152, 153
Leader 85, 113, 149
Learning 13, 14, 25, 26, 50, 126, 127, 134
Level of commitment 29, 30, 150
Listener 18, 20
Listening 15, 127, 152
Love 47, 88, 122, 128, 140, 142, 150, 152, 153

M

Mentor 16, 17, 18, 19, 20, 121, 141, 147, 150, 151, 152
Mentoring relationships 19, 21
Mentors 13, 18, 19, 22, 57, 151
Mountain 38, 39, 40, 41, 42, 72, 73, 77

N

Network 55, 56, 57, 97, 102, 108, 109, 110, 124, 132
Networking 57, 111, 124

O

Open organizations 94, 95, 97
Opportunities 16, 28, 31, 45, 47, 110, 124, 133
Opportunity 10, 15, 19, 37, 42, 45, 69, 71, 72, 79, 109, 110, 115,
    118, 140, 141, 143
Outer-directed 139, 144
Outsider 13, 51, 118

P

Panju 115, 117, 118
Panjus 115, 117, 118, 119, 129

Bibliography

Forsyth, Adrian and Ken Miyata. *Tropical Nature: Life and Death in the Rain Forests of Central and South America*. New York: Macmillan, 1984.

Loden, Marily and Judy B. Rosener. *Workforce America: Managing Employee Diversity as a Vital Resource*. Donnelley, 1991.

Nowak, Ronald M. Walkers. *Mammals of the World*, Volume II. Baltimore and London: John's Hopkins University Press, 1991.

Plotkin, Mark J. *Tales of a Shaman's Apprentice*. New York: Viking, 1993.

Thomas, R. Roosevelt, Jr. with Tracy Irving Gray, Jr. and Marjorie Woodruff. *Differences Do Make a Difference*. Atlanta, Georgia: American Institute for Managing Diversity, 1992.

Wassman, Thomas; Frohlich, Hans Joseph; et al. *The Plight of the Tropical Rainforest: Vanishing Eden*. editor North American Edition: Edward G. Atkins, Ph.D. Hauppage, New York: Barron's Educational Series, 1991.

About the Author

Shirley Peddy, Ph.D., is Managing Director of learningconnections, a business consulting firm based in Corpus Christi, Texas. Her extensive knowledge of organizational effectiveness, communication, diversity and training comes from twenty years as an internal consultant and leader of a training organization within Exxon USA, where she organized and worked with a world-wide advisory committee. Her communication background includes being on the faculty of Louisiana State University where she taught honors English, and serving as Chairman of the English Department, Dominican College, Houston, Texas. She is an award-winning training designer and has spoken at numerous national conferences. Her primary areas of expertise include communication, coaching, career development, mentoring, team building, leadership training and conflict resolution. She has conducted workshops all over the United States and in foreign countries.

Order Form

Please send the following books:
I understand that I may return any books for a full refund—for any reason, no questions asked.

_____ copies *Secrets of the Jungle* @ $14.95 each   Sub-Total: _____

Please add 8.25% for books shipped to Texas addresses   Sales Tax: _____

Shipping rate: $4.00 for the first book and $1.00 for   Shipping: _____
each additional book to the same address

Total: _____

Colleges, Universities, Quantity Buyers:
Discounts on this book are available for bulk purchases. Write or call for information on our discount programs.

Mailing Address:
Name: _____

Address: _____

_____

City: _____ State: _____ Zip: _____

Payment:

☐ Check

☐ Credit Card   ____ **VISA.**   ____ **MasterCard** ®

Card Number _____

Name on Card _____ *(please print)*

Expiration Date _____ / _____

Signature _____

Telephone orders: (800) 460-4038 (24 hours a day)

Postal orders: **Publication Services, Inc.**
8870 Business Park Drive
Austin, Texas 78759

Order Form

Please send the following books:
I understand that I may return any books for a full refund—for any reason, no questions asked.

_____ copies *Secrets of the Jungle* @ $14.95 each   Sub-Total: _____

Please add 8.25% for books shipped to Texas addresses   Sales Tax: _____

Shipping rate: $4.00 for the first book and $1.00 for   Shipping: _____
    each additional book to the same address

                                                                              Total: _____

Colleges, Universities, Quantity Buyers:
Discounts on this book are available for bulk purchases. Write or call for information on our discount programs.

Mailing Address:
Name: _____

Address: _____

_____

City: _____ State: _____ Zip: _____

Payment:

☐ Check

☐ Credit Card   ____ **VISA.**   ____ **MasterCard** ®

Card Number _____

Name on Card _____ *(please print)*

Expiration Date _____ / _____

Signature _____

Telephone orders: (800) 460-4038 (24 hours a day)

Postal orders: Publication Services, Inc.
8870 Business Park Drive
Austin, Texas 78759

learningconnections provides a full range of consulting and training services for business, government and educational organizations focusing on leadership, team building, careers, coaching and communication.

We can help you build a more capable, more productive and more empowering organization through increasing the contributions of people.

For information about consulting, workshops, custom on-site programs and seminars, and speaking engagements:

learningconnections
14225 SPID, Ste 10-337
Corpus Christi, TX 78418

(512) 949-8309 – phone
(512) 949-8331 – fax